FLOYD CLYMER'S MOTORCYCLIST'S LIBRARY

BOOK OF THE B.S.A.

A COMPLETE GUIDE FOR OWNERS
AND PROSPECTIVE PURCHASERS
OF B.S.A. MACHINES

Written by an independent owner-driver, dealing with every phase of motor-cycling from the registration to selling of the machine second-hand. Including chapters on Driving, Touring, Legal Matters, Insurance, Overhauling.

BY

"WAYSIDER"

SECOND EDITION
1926

ANNOUNCEMENT

By special arrangement with the original publishers of this book, Sir Isaac Pitman & Son, Ltd., of London, England, we have secured the exclusive publishing rights for this book, as well as all others in THE MOTORCYCLIST'S LIBRARY.

Included in THE MOTORCYCLIST'S LIBRARY are complete instruction manuals covering the care and operation of respective motorcycles and engines; valuable data on speed tuning, and thrilling accounts of motorcycle race events. See listing of available titles elsewhere in this edition.

We consider it a privilege to be able to offer so many fine titles to our customers.

FLOYD CLYMER
Publisher of Books Pertaining to Automobiles and Motorcycles
2125 W. PICO ST.   LOS ANGELES 6, CALIF.

INTRODUCTION

Welcome to the world of digital publishing ~ the book you now hold in your hand, while unchanged from the original edition, was printed using the latest state of the art digital technology. The advent of print-on-demand has forever changed the publishing process, never has information been so accessible and it is our hope that this book serves your informational needs for years to come. If this is your first exposure to digital publishing, we hope that you are pleased with the results. Many more titles of interest to the classic automobile and motorcycle enthusiast, collector and restorer are available via our website at www.VelocePress.com. We hope that you find this title as interesting as we do.

NOTE FROM THE PUBLISHER

The information presented is true and complete to the best of our knowledge. All recommendations are made without any guarantees on the part of the author or the publisher, who also disclaim all liability incurred with the use of this information.

TRADEMARKS

We recognize that some words, model names and designations, for example, mentioned herein are the property of the trademark holder. We use them for identification purposes only. This is not an official publication.

INFORMATION ON THE USE OF THIS PUBLICATION

This manual is an invaluable resource for the classic motorcycle enthusiast and a "must have" for owners interested in performing their own maintenance. However, in today's information age we are constantly subject to changes in common practice, new technology, availability of improved materials and increased awareness of chemical toxicity. As such, it is advised that the user consult with an experienced professional prior to undertaking any procedure described herein. While every care has been taken to ensure correctness of information, it is obviously not possible to guarantee complete freedom from errors or omissions or to accept liability arising from such errors or omissions. Therefore, any individual that uses the information contained within, or elects to perform or participate in do-it-yourself repairs or modifications acknowledges that there is a risk factor involved and that the publisher or its associates cannot be held responsible for personal injury or property damage resulting from the use of the information or the outcome of such procedures.

WARNING!

One final word of advice, this publication is intended to be used as a reference guide, and when in doubt the reader should consult with a qualified technician.

PREFACE

THE second edition of this volume has afforded me an opportunity of bringing it up to date, of amplifying matters which correspondence has shown me to be necessary, and of adding matter which correspondents have suggested would render the work of greater value.

The main development in B.S.A. machines during the past two years has been in the introduction of grease-gun lubrication to all models except the 2·49 standard model, of all-chain drive to all models, and of De Luxe models having refinements in the way of footboards, special saddles, and larger-section tyres.

" WAYSIDER."

PREFACE TO THE FIRST EDITION

THIS handbook is intended as a work of reference for those who already possess or propose to buy one of the eleven different B.S.A. mounts, and also as a general treatise on the equipment, running, overhaul, and simple repair of motor-cycles. It will also, it is hoped, be found useful by others who wish to obtain reliable and unbiased information regarding this popular type of motor-cycle.

It will readily be apparent that much of the information is of a general character, and applies equally well to other makes. Carburation, for example, is a subject on which information cannot be said to apply to any one make. Where, however, details of practice differ, those details as applicable only to B.S.A. mounts are dealt with separately.

The chapters on Preliminaries and Driving should be read through before the machine is taken on the road.

A question of some importance to every owner, sooner or later, is the disposal of the old mount, and space is devoted in this book to that special subject. Even in such a simple matter there are pitfalls to be avoided, and the information given is designed to show how to get the most for the old machine.

It is hoped that the general instructions on faults and their remedies will be helpful; they are the result of practical experience. Should, however, any special difficulty arise, in spite of the effort which has been made to cater for all possible contingencies, the reader has only to address a letter to " Waysider," c/o The Publishers (enclosing a stamped envelope), to receive helpful advice in the course of a post or so. It is only fair to add that the author of this book has no past or present connection whatsoever with the B.S.A., to whom, however, he is indebted for valuable assistance and for permission to reproduce several of the illustrations.

" WAYSIDER."

Get your B.S.A. from
THE B.S.A. SPECIALISTS

We have the largest stock of B.S.A.'s in the Midlands and can give
IMMEDIATE DELIVERY
of any of the 15 B.S.A. Models

OUR DEFERRED PAYMENTS
are arranged to suit individual requirements

OUR EXCHANGE ALLOWANCES
are more liberal than elsewhere

We have the largest representative stock of B.S.A. Spares in this Country. We invite all B.S.A. riders to write for the official B.S.A. Spares Catalogue, sent free, and to avail themselves of our unique Registered Service.

THE B.S.A. SPECIALISTS
300 & 301 BROAD STREET, BIRMINGHAM

Telephone: Midland 2670   Grams: "Comocyco, B'ham"

CONTENTS

CHAP.		PAGE
	PREFACE	
I.	THE VARIOUS B.S.A. MOUNTS	1
II.	REGISTRATION, DRIVING LICENCE AND EQUIPMENT	14
III.	DRIVING	18
IV.	HOW THE ENGINE WORKS	35
V.	MECHANICAL DETAILS OF THE B.S.A.	41
VI.	OVERHAULING	63
VII.	RUNNING COSTS	76
VIII.	TOURING	81
IX.	FAULTS : THEIR LOCATION AND REMEDY	88
X.	LEGAL MATTERS	98
XI.	BUYING AND SELLING AN OLD MOUNT	102
XII.	USEFUL INFORMATION	105
	SUPPLEMENT - 1927 BSA MODELS	111
	INDEX	115

For your B.S.A.

BUY Mobiloil in the sealed quart can at practically the price of oil from bulk. Mobiloil "BB" in summer and Mobiloil "TT" (Improved) in winter are recommendations which are endorsed by the Birmingham Small Arms Co., Ltd.

"Correct Lubrication for Motor Cycles" is an authoritative booklet which every motor-cyclist should possess. Send for a post-free copy to-day.

Mobiloil
Make the chart your guide

VACUUM OIL COMPANY, LTD., LONDON, S.W.1

ILLUSTRATIONS

FIG.		PAGE
1.	The 2·49 h.p. Lightweight	1
2.	The 3·49 h.p. Side Valve Model	2
3.	The 3·49 h.p. Overhead Valve Model	2
4.	The 4·93 h.p. Model	4
5.	The 2·49 h.p. De Luxe Model	4
6.	The 5·57 h.p. Model	5
7.	The 5·57 h.p. Model with Box Carrier	7
8.	The 3·49 h.p. Lightweight Motor-cycle with " Skiff " Sidecar	7
9.	The 7·70 h.p. Light Model	7
10.	The 9·86 h.p. De Luxe Model	8
11.	The B.S.A. Sidecar Model No. 6	9
12.	The B.S.A. Light Sidecar Model No. 7	9
13.	The B.S.A. Sidecar Model No. 7a	9
14.	The B.S.A. Sidecar Model No. 8	11
15.	The B.S.A. Tradesman's Box Carrier	12
16.	The B.S.A. Commercial Van Sidecar	12
17.	Conventional Road Signs	28
18.	How to Warn Following Traffic that you are About to Turn to Left or Right	29
19.	Warning Following Traffic that you are About to Stop	31
20.	The Principle of the Four-stroke Engine	36
21.	Diagram showing Relation between Petrol Level and Jet, etc.	38
22.	Position of Armature, etc.	39
23.	Section of Cylinder Head 3·49 o.h.v. Engine	42
24.	The 3·49 h.p. Overhead Valve Cylinder Head	43
25.	The 3·49 h.p. Overhead Valve Engine Valve—Gear Side	44
26. 27.	What your Engine looks like Inside	45
28.	The Cam-faced Cush Drive, etc.	46
29.	The Aluminium Piston and the Cast Iron Piston	47
30. 31.	Two-speed Gear Box, 2·49 h.p. Motor-cycle	48
32. 33.	The Three-speed Gear Box	50

ILLUSTRATIONS

FIG.		PAGE
34.	The B.S.A. Plate Clutch	53
35.	Detail View of 3·49 h.p. Model	54
36.	The Lubricating System of the B.S.A.	55
37.	The Important Parts Requiring Lubrication	56
38.	Cut-away View of Amac Carburettor	57
39.	Details of the Front Fork on the 3·49 h.p. Models	58
40.	Cut-away Detail View of the 5·57 h.p. Engine	59
41.	The Detachable Wheel	60
42.	The Disc Adjusting Hub, for Rapid Chain Adjustment	61
43.	Diagram showing how to Adjust the Tappets	64
44.	How to Remove Piston Rings	65
45.	Diagram showing how Valves become Pocketed after frequent Regrinding	67
46.	The Make-and-break Portion of the Magneto	68
47.	How to Adjust the Front Chain	69
48.	How to Align the Sidecar	72
49. } 50. }	The Correct and Incorrect Methods of Coiling Petrol Pipes.	73
51.	How to Remove Studs	74
52.	An Excellent Method of Checking Tyre Pressure by means of Two Cards	76
53.	Diagram Illustrating Reach of Sparking Plug.	78
54.	Wiring Diagrams for Electric Lights	79

BOOK OF THE B.S.A.

CHAPTER 1

THE VARIOUS B.S.A. MOUNTS

THIRTEEN different B.S.A. motor-cycles are marketed, ranging from 2·49 h.p. to 9·86 h.p.—two 2·49 h.p., two 3·49 h.p., two 4·93 h.p., two 5·57 h.p., two 7·70 h.p., and three 9·86 h.p. These, however, really represent seven designs, some of the models also

FIG. 1.—THE 2·49 H.P. LIGHTWEIGHT

being supplied with refinements, these chiefly consisting of a Terry spring saddle, footrests, aluminium chain cases (to the 9·86, 7·70, and 5·57 models only), Dunlop extra heavy tyres. In a book of this nature, specifications are unavoidable, and are here presented as fully as possible in order, beginning with the lowest powered machine.

The 2·49 h.p. Model. This machine is a recent introduction to the B.S.A. range, and is intended to provide a machine light in weight, easy to handle, having a good road speed for touring, and, in conjunction with the B.S.A. two-speed gear box, sufficient power to surmount all reasonable hills which may be encountered. It is, therefore, a machine which is at once cheap, light, handy, ideal for traffic, and economical in use. Whilst its speed and power will not disappoint the most experienced rider, it is so light and simple to handle that the novice, the lady, or the middle-aged man, who might feel nervous with the larger machines, will find this one almost as easy to ride and handle as the bicycle. It is shown by Fig. 1, and the specification is as follows—

ENGINE. This is a single cylinder of 2·49 h.p., 63 mm. bore × 80 mm. stroke, making it of 249 c.c., or 2·49 h.p. (according to

FIG. 2.—THE 3·49 H.P. SIDE VALVE MODEL

A.C.U. rating, which assumes 100 c.c. to equal 1 h.p.). It has a piston of aluminium alloy and a roller big-end bearing, whilst the

FIG. 3.—THE 3·49 H.P. OVERHEAD VALVE MODEL

engine mainshaft (driving side) is mounted on ball bearings; the gear side of the shaft runs in a plain bearing, an arrangement quite consistent with engineering practice. The valves are of large area (large area is desirable, for it prevents the valve faces becoming pitted, as well as minimizing wear and ensuring a lengthy effective life of the faces before grinding in is necessary) and of alloy steel, both valves being mechanically operated.

THE VARIOUS B.S.A. MOUNTS

Back pressure is avoided by the provision of a large silencer and exhaust pipe. The timing gear is comparatively silent.

CARBURETTOR AND IGNITION. An Amac carburettor is fitted, and the handlebar-controlled ball bearing magneto is driven by gears enclosed in an oil-tight aluminium case. The magneto is of the "all weather" type, provision being made by suitable covers for the exclusion of dust and water.

THE FRAME AND FORKS. It is conceded that a frame should have a low riding position (and hence a low centre-of-gravity), and the frame is so made, being constructed of weldless steel tubing and steel lugs. The new B.S.A. spring fork is provided, this being fitted with barrel-shaped compression spring and efficiently lubricated link bearings.

BRAKES, WHEELS AND TYRES. The two brakes provided operate independently on a brake rim mounted on the rear wheel; one is actuated by a lever fixed to the right side of handlebar, the other by toe-pedal on the right side of the machine. The wheels are 24 in. $\times$ 2¼ in., taking tyres of similar size. They are enamelled, and have waterproof and dustproof hubs. As sent out the wheels are equipped with Dunlop 3-ply tyres.

TANK. This is of circular cross-section, is fixed to the top tube and front down tube, and is detachable. It is provided with bayonet-jointed safety-chain filler caps of the unleakable type, and its capacity is 1½ gallons of petrol and 2¼ pints of oil.

TRANSMISSION. Roller chains of ½ in. pitch (special heavy type) are used throughout; the front drive is enclosed in a chain case, and the rear drive is protected by a guard. A special device is fitted to the engine shaft to obtain a smooth transmission of power. For gear ratios see page 52. The clutch is contained in the large chain wheel, and is of the floating dry-plate type controlled by a lever on the left-hand side of the handlebar.

The B.S.A. 2-speed gear box is fitted. This is of the constant mesh type. The kick-starter mechanism is enclosed in the gear box. Change speed lever is on the right-hand side of the machine, with the selector quadrant fixed on the gear box, so that the position of lever can be readily seen.

LUBRICATION. Gravity feed to mechanical pump, then to sight feed on tank, and feeding to crank-case. Hand pump is also fitted for emergency use.

MISCELLANEOUS DETAILS. A back stand (kick up) and front stand are fitted. Footrests are adjustable to 12 positions, footboards being an extra. The excellent mudguarding of B.S.A. machines also characterizes this mount, and is of wide, plain section. Handlebars are of touring or of semi-sporting type, both types being adjustable. A detachable tubular carrier, metal celluloid covered inflator, tool-bag and tool-roll completes the equipment. The finish consists of four coats of black enamel, bright parts plated. It is important to note that the weight is only 180 lb., a cogent matter from the point of view of taxation, and in the chapter dealing with that subject the point is fully explained.

FIG. 4.—THE 4·93 H.P. MODEL

FIG. 5.—THE 2·49 H.P. DE LUXE MODEL

The 2·49 h.p. De Luxe Model has a black and gold tank, three-speed gear box, Terry saddle, grease-gun lubrication, and 24 in. × 3½ in. 3-ply tyres. These are the only important respects in which it differs from the other 2¼ h.p. model. The De Luxe weighs 185 lb.

The 3·49 h.p. Side Valve Model (shown by Fig. 2) was first produced in November, 1922, and to the sporting solo rider who asks for a " go anywhere " mount its records in the Scottish Six Days' Trials and the International Trials in Sweden in 1923 stand as recommendation. It is produced with equipment to suit either the sporting man or the tourist. The machine is not

THE VARIOUS B.S.A. MOUNTS

designed for sidecar work, but will carry a pillion passenger, and is a popular machine.

ENGINE. Single cylinder 3·49 h.p., 72 mm. bore × 85½ mm. stroke, making 349 c.c. or 3·49 h.p. according to A.C.U. rating. Roller big-end bearing; engine mainshaft (driving side) mounted on roller bearing, plain bearing on gear side. Large special alloy steel valves are provided, both mechanically operated, as well as an aluminium alloy piston, silent timing gear, large exhaust pipe and silencer.

CARBURETTOR AND IGNITION. The magneto is a high-tension ball-bearing weatherproof type, with handlebar control, and driven by adjustable chain in aluminium dust-proof case. The carburettor is an Amac.

FIG. 6.—THE 5·57 H.P. MODEL

FRAME AND FORKS. The frame is constructed to give a low riding position, and the spring fork is a new type of B.S.A., fitted with a taper compression spring and link bearings.

BRAKES, WHEELS AND TYRES. A front brake is fitted, operating on a brake rim, and not on the rim of the wheel; it is applied by means of the lever on the right-hand side of the handlebar. The rear brake is provided with a parallel-motion shoe acting on the brake rim mounted on the rear wheel and operated by a toe pedal on the right side of the machine. The wheels have flat base rims, are 26 in. × 2¼ in., enamelled and fitted with Dunlop heavy tyres. The hubs are waterproof and dustproof.

TANK. This is supported on brackets brazed to the frame, and is quickly detachable. Filler caps (unleakable) are secured by means of bayonet joint and chain. A combined priming and petrol tap is fitted, unleakable cork-faced. Capacity for petrol, 1½ gallons, oil 2½ pints.

TRANSMISSION. Roller chains (⅝ in. × ¼ in.) are used throughout. Front drive is enclosed in chain case, and rear drive is protected by a guard. The anti-shock device is fitted to the engine shaft. For gear ratios see page 52.

The clutch is contained in the large chain wheel, and is of the floating dry-plate type, controlled like the 2·49 h.p. machine, from the left handlebar. The B.S.A. 3-speed gear box is provided. All gears are constantly in mesh. The kick-starter mechanism is enclosed in the gear box, and the change-speed lever is on the right side of the tank.

MISCELLANEOUS DETAILS. The back stand is of the kick up style, fixed to the chain-stay end, designed with a special lug to prevent side play, and engages underneath the chain stay end. When not in use it is securely fixed to the rear mudguard by a spring clip. A front stand also is fitted.

LUBRICATION. Gravity feed to mechanical pump, then to sight feed on tank, feeding to crankcase. Hand pump is also fitted for emergency use. Hubs, forks, and links, etc., are fitted with grease-gun nipples.

Twelve-position adjustable footrests, detachable tubular carrier, inflator, tool-bag and tool-roll, wide plain-section mudguards, touring handlebars (or sporting with rubber grips) and finish as for the 2·49 h.p. machine completes the specification. The weight is 225 lb.

3·49 h.p. Overhead Valve De Luxe Model.

This model, shown by Fig. 3, differs from the preceding one in that it is equipped with an overhead valve engine. The valve gear is enclosed and automatically lubricated. It is not designed for sidecar work, but will carry a pillion passenger.

ENGINE. This is of the same proportion as the S.V. engine—that is 72 mm. bore by 85½ mm. stroke, making 349 c.c. or 3·49 h.p. at A.C.U. rating. It has a roller big-end bearing, and the engine mainshaft (driving side) is mounted on a roller bearing, a plain bearing being fitted on the gear side. An accessible detachable head fitted with overhead valves and compound valve springs is embodied, valves being operated by phosphor bronze bushed rockers, equipped with felt oiling rings, working on hardened-steel pins. All valve gear is enclosed and automatically lubricated by oil mist from the crankcase, forced up the push rod casings to the rocker boxes by crankcase compression. The piston is of aluminium alloy, and the exhaust system is plated, and having a large tail pipe, giving mellow note at all speeds, without loss of efficiency. A special Amac carburettor is fitted, and 26 in. × 2½ in. beaded Dunlop tyres.

The weight is 243 lb.

THE VARIOUS B.S.A. MOUNTS

Fig. 7.—The 5·57 h.p. Model with Box Carrier

Fig. 8.—The 3·49 h.p. Model with "Skiff" Sidecar

Fig. 9.—The 7·70 h.p. Light Model

4·93 h.p. Sports Model. The 500 c.c. machine still holds the affections of a large body of motor-cyclists. It provides the sporting rider with a fast touring mount for both solo and passenger work, and the 4·93 h.p. B.S.A. has been produced specially to meet this demand. Whilst the 4·93 h.p. Sports B.S.A. machine (see Fig. 4) is capable of high speeds, it does not profess to be tuned for track racing, but it maintains its " tune " for thousands of miles. It is recommended that a B.S.A. sidecar No. 7 or 7a be fitted for touring, and for this purpose 700 mm. × 80 mm. tyres will be fitted if desired, but at extra cost.

THE ENGINE is a single cylinder, 4·93 h.p., 80 mm. × 98 mm. bore and stroke (493 c.c., or 4·93 h.p.), and has a roller big-end

FIG. 10.—THE 9·86 H.P. DE LUXE MODEL

bearing, mainshaft mounted on extra large ball bearings, large special alloy steel valves, both mechanically operated. Decompressor to facilitate starting. Aluminium alloy piston.

CARBURETTOR AND IGNITION. Same specification as for 3·49 h.p. Overhead Valve model.

FRAME AND FORKS. A special sporting frame is incorporated, and front and rear sidecar attachments are built integral with the frame. The barrel-spring type of front fork is provided.

BRAKES, WHEELS AND TYRES. Braking is by rim fitted to the front wheel (operating lever on right handlebar), the rear brake being a parallel-motion shoe, acting by means of a toe pedal (not toe pedal, as with 3·49 h.p. models) on a rim fixed to the back wheel. The toe pedal is on the right-hand side of the machine.

Wheels are flat base rims, 650 mm. × 65 mm. fitted with Dunlop tyres.

TANK. Same as 3·49 h.p. models, but with capacity for 1½ gallons of petrol and 2½ pints of oil.

THE VARIOUS B.S.A. MOUNTS

Fig. 11.—The B.S.A. Sidecar, Model No. 6

Fig. 12.—The B.S.A. Light Sidecar, Model No. 7

Fig. 13.—The B.S.A. Sidecar, Model No. 7a

MISCELLANEOUS DETAILS. The transmission, clutch, gear box, stands, lubrication, equipment and finish are identical with the specification already noted with regard to the 3·49 S.V. model. The front mudguard, it should be noted, has a splash attachment. The weight is 259 lb. (De Luxe weighs 273 lb.) and the price as for the 3·49 O.H.V. model.

5·57 h.p. Model with Countershaft Gear.

The more expensive models in this class provide additional refinements. Sidecars Nos. 6, 7 and 7a are suitable for this mount, and for the two other 4¼ h.p. models.

ENGINE. Single cylinder 4¼ h.p., 85 mm. × 98 mm. bore and stroke (557 c.c., or 5·57 h.p.). Roller big-end bearing, mainshaft mounted on extra large ball bearings. Large special alloy steel valves, both mechanically operated. Decompressor to facilitate starting. Silent timing gear, large capacity silencer.

TANK. Same as already noted, but with 2⅛ gallons petrol capacity and 3 pints of oil.

FRAME AND FORKS. Integral sidecar attachments and barrel-type spring forks.

TRANSMISSION. ⅝ in. × ⅜ in. roller chain from engine to gear box, with chain case and chain guard, which is quickly detachable. Dunlop 1 in. belt over 7⅜ in. diameter pulley to rear wheel. Engine fitted with 16 tooth sprocket as standard. For gear ratios see page 52.

BRAKES, WHEELS AND TYRES. 650 mm. × 65 mm. Dunlop heavy wired tyres, brakes same as 4·93 h.p. model, but operated by heel pedal on right-hand side.

MISCELLANEOUS DETAILS. Handlebars of touring, semi-T.T. or sporting pattern are fitted. The back stand is kick up, fixed on a solid boss on the chain stay end and supported by a strut engaging with the underside of the chain stay tube. When not in use it is securely fixed to the rear mudguard by a spring clip. Front stand is also fitted. The cycle parts are lubricated by grease-gun.

Lubrication and other details not specifically mentioned here are as for the 4·93 h.p. model, and equipment is, of course, provided.

The weight is 290 lb., and grease-gun lubrication is fitted.

5·57 h.p. De Luxe All Chain Model.

This has 26 in. × 3 in. Dunlop heavy tyres fitted to 650 mm. × 65 mm. wheels, disc-adjusting hubs, tank capacity of 2¼ gallons of petrol and 3 pints of oil, and weighs 313 lb. A Terry spring saddle is fitted, foot-boards replace footrests, 26 in. × 3¼ in. wired-on tyres are fitted, the wheels are quickly detachable and interchangeable, and the

THE VARIOUS B.S.A. MOUNTS

transmission is entirely enclosed in aluminium chain cases. (See Fig. 7.)

7·70 h.p. Twin with Countershaft Gear. Although the present trend is to make all large twin-cylinder machines almost solely passenger vehicles, it is interesting to note that the 7·70 h.p. model provides an easily handled solo machine for those experienced riders who find a fascination in the big reserve of power and feeling of road supremacy, coupled with the smooth running that can only be obtained from machines of this class.

FIG. 14.—THE B.S.A. SIDECAR, MODEL NO. 8

Two 7·70 h.p. models are marketed, one having only the rear wheel detachable, the other two having interchangeable wheels, one of the latter two is the De Luxe model. They are adapted for use with a full touring outfit, which may be, and often is, required to take extra loads and yet maintain a high average speed.

Sidecars Nos. 6, 7, 7a and 8 are recommended for the 7·70 h.p, mounts.

ENGINE. Twin cylinder 7·70 h.p. (770 c.c.), 76 mm. × 85 mm. bore and stroke, mainshaft mounted on ball bearings. Very large special steel and mechanically operated valves. Improved adjustable tappets. Simplified timing gear. Big-end bearings fitted with rollers. Pistons fitted with patent gudgeon pin. Improved distribution of oil to front cylinder. Design of inlet pipe obviates air leak and trouble in fitting.

FRAME AND FORK. Integral sidecar fittings to frame, and barrel type spring forks are embodied.

BRAKES, WHEELS AND TYRES. The front brake is of the brake-rim and shoe type, so arranged that detachability of the front wheel is not interfered with. The rear brake is as on the other models, and heel operated. Wheels, which are interchangeable, are fitted with 26 in. × 3 in. or 26 in. × 3¼ in. wired-on Dunlop heavy tyres, and disc-adjusting hubs.

Fig. 15.—The B.S.A. Tradesman's Box Carrier

Fig. 16.—The B.S.A. Commercial Van Sidecar

Lubrication by mechanical oil pump, enclosed in timing gear case, fed through sight feed lubricator. Hand pump is also fitted for use in emergency. Grease-gun lubrication to the cycle parts.

Transmission. ⅝ in. × ⅜ in. roller chains; front drive enclosed in oiltight aluminium chain case and rear drive protected by an excellent guard. For gear ratios see page 52.

Miscellaneous Details. Capacity of petrol tank is 2½ gallons of spirit to 3 pints of oil. Silencer has two outlet pipes, footboards are provided. Other details, equipment, etc., as for 5·57 h.p. machine. Weight is 320 lb.

7·70 h.p. Twin De Luxe. This model differs from the preceding machine in detail only. The pistons are fitted with patent gudgeon pins, it has a Terry spring seat, in place of the usual type of saddle, and it weighs 338 lb. (See Fig. 9.) The patent gudgeon pins are fitted to 5·57, 7·70, and 9·86 h.p. models. Footboards are fitted in place of footrests, the wheels are quickly detachable and interchangeable, and an aluminium chain case is fitted.

9·86 h.p. Twin with Countershaft Gear. This model (Fig. 10) has an 80 mm. bore × 98 mm. (986 c.c., or 9·86 h.p.) stroke engine, and capacity for 3½ pints of oil, the details otherwise being identical with the 7·70 h.p. machine. It weighs 334 lb. Sidecars Nos. 6, 7, 7a and 8 are advised.

The more expensive models of the 5·57 h.p., 7·70 h.p. and 9·86 h.p. machines provide the additional refinements of totally enclosed lubricated transmission, a special spring saddle, and the facility of detachable and interchangeable wheels. The inscriptions to Figs. 11 to 16 are self-explanatory.

The 8 h.p. De Luxe and 8 h.p. Colonial models (weights 348 lb. and 353 lb. respectively) have the same refinements as the other De Luxe models—that is to say, footrests, Terry saddles, and 26 in. × 3¼ in. wired-on tyres. The 8 h.p. De Luxe has an aluminium chain case.

CHAPTER II

REGISTRATION, DRIVING LICENCE AND EQUIPMENT

IN this chapter, the writer pre-supposes that the reader, having selected his mount to suit his inclinations, now turns to the question of the necessary legal formalities and requirements to be satisfied before the machine can take to the road. All matters which are compulsory—like income-tax—are distasteful; some of the regulations relating to motor-cycles may appear ambiguous, but nevertheless they cannot be disregarded, and to indicate flaws in the law does not absolve one from responsibility. Firstly, then, regarding the driving licence.

The Driving Licence. This licence must be in the possession of all drivers of motor vehicles when driving, and it must be produced when the request is made by a police officer. The mere possession of the licence, be it noted, does not discharge liability, for it must be carried whilst driving the vehicle. *It may not be lent* to any person for the purpose of driving the owner's machine. As the law stands at present, any person can obtain a driving licence. The licence, therefore, is no indication of ability, but merely an index or receipt for tax paid. It is procurable from the local Borough or County Council office, and it costs 5s. per year, the year counting from the date on which the licence is issued until the corresponding date of the subsequent year. There is no need to apply personally for it—application may be made by post—but personal application saves time, especially if an entry on the official application form is likely to be queried. If the reader is over seventeen years of age, it is best to make application for a licence to drive a motor-car, which entitles the holder to drive either motor-car or motor-cycle, whereas a driving licence applying to motor-cycles alone restricts the holder to that type of vehicle. If the reader at the time of application is under seventeen, he may only apply for a motor-cycle driver's licence, but in any case he must be over fourteen years of age.

Registration and Tax. All motor-cycles must be registered at the local Borough or County Council office, and if the machine is to be used on the public roads a tax must be paid on it; a part of the application form is given on page 15, showing the amount.

It will be seen that the licence may be taken out quarterly. For the purpose of the law, the term *weight unladen* is taken to

REGISTRATION, DRIVING LICENCE, ETC.

mean the machine in its running condition, and does not include the tool kit, petrol, accumulators, or water. The licence (a circular label on which is entered details of machine, date, and amount of tax paid) must be exhibited in a conspicuous position on the near-side (left-hand side facing the front) of the machine, and be carried in a weather-proof holder with transparent front

I apply for a licence expiring on 192 , for a: MOTOR-CYCLE (or motor scooter or cycle with auto-wheel or other motor attachment: Note: Motor-cycles exceeding 8 cwt. in weight unladen are chargeable to duty as cars.	Annual Licences expiring on 31st December.	Quarterly licences expiring on 24th March, 30th June, 30th Sept. or 31st December.
	Duty. £ s. d.	Duty. £ s. d.
(a) Bicycle:—		
Weight unladen, not exceeding 200 lb.	1 10 –	8 3
Weight unladen, not exceeding 200 lb. with right to draw trailer or sidecar	2 10 –	13 9
Weight unladen exceeding 200 lb., but not exceeding 8 cwt.	3 – –	16 6
Weight unladen exceeding 200 lb. with right to draw trailer or sidecar	4 – –	1 2 –
(b) Tricycle (not exceeding 8 cwt. in weight unladen	4 – –	1 2 –

so as clearly to be visible by daylight to a person standing at the near side of the vehicle.

A registration book is issued with the licence, and in it is entered full particulars of the machine, as well as conditions of renewal of the licence. When selling the machine this registration book should be sent to the registration authority, who effects its transference to the new owner, and *both vendor and purchaser must notify the registration authority of the transaction.* This form of registration serves a useful purpose in that when buying a second-hand machine one has, in the registration book, a sort of history of the machine. Every licence now has a surrender value; for details apply to the issuing council. If the licence is renewed at the end of the first or second quarter, the amount payable will be three times or twice the quarterly amount, as the case may be.

Number Plates. This simple item of the equipment is hedged round with restrictions. One must be provided at the front and rear of the machine, and upon them must be painted the registered numbers which have been assigned to the machine and which are entered on the registration label and also in the registration book. The numbers must conform to the following proportions : Each figure or letter must be at least $1\frac{3}{4}$ in. by $1\frac{1}{4}$ in. wide, and $\frac{5}{16}$ in.

thick at all parts. Between the top and bottom of the letters and the edge of the plate there must be a margin of at least ¼ in., with a margin of ½ in. at each side. The letters must be in white on a black ground, and they must not be permitted to become obscured by mud or dust; nor must the view of them be obstructed by any person or article on the machine. The legal aspects of the matter are more fully discussed in a subsequent chapter.

Lamps. During the period between one hour after sunset and one hour before sunrise (see time table on page 87) it is compulsory to show a white light at the front of the machine and, in the case of a combination, a red light at the rear. One number plate must be illuminated—it does not matter whether front or rear. If the machine is a combination this also must have a lamp showing white forward, and it must be fixed in such a way that from the front and in conjunction with the headlamp it fairly indicates the extreme width of the vehicle. An Act is at present before Parliament which seeks to make it compulsory for all motor-cycles (as well as cycles) to have a red rear light.

Audible Warning of Approach. A horn, either of the mechanical or the bulb type, must be fitted so that adequate and audible warning of approach may be given to pedestrians, as well as to the drivers of other vehicles. Preference is given to a bulb horn yielding a deep, sonorous note.

It may be taken that legal matters regarding the machine itself, such as silencing, brakes, etc., have been attended to by the makers, and there is little need to reiterate such regulations here. The chapter on legal matters, however, deals with the question of breach of them.

JOINING A CLUB

There can be no question that many advantages may be derived from joining either the A.C.U. (Auto-Cycle Union), the A.A. (Automobile Association), or the R.A.C. (Royal Automobile Club). Free legal advice and defence, " get-you-home " scheme, services of road guides and local consuls, touring and technical assistance, and insurance facilities are available for a nominal annual subscription. The addresses of the above clubs are given hereunder—

Auto-Cycle Union,	Royal Automobile Club,
83 Pall Mall,	89-91 Pall Mall,
London, S.W.1.	London, S.W.1.
Automobile Association and Motor Union,	and
66-68 Whitcomb Street,	7 and 8 New Coventry Street,
London, W.C.2 ;	London, W.1.

REGISTRATION, DRIVING LICENCE, ETC. 17

and application should be made to the secretary in each case for the necessary form. If a local club is affiliated to one of these bodies, it is better perhaps to join the local club, the fee to the latter covering the fee to the former, whilst one enjoys membership of both. If one intends to go in for competition work, and enter for the various contests organized by the bodies mentioned, membership is absolutely necessary.

INSURANCE

It is not compulsory for one to insure against loss by fire, personal injury by accident, injury to others (third party risks), injury to machine, loss of machine by theft, but it is beyond all cavil that it is wise to do so. Loss by fire or theft affect the rider only to the extent of the value of the machine, and are matters of less importance than those of injury. Indeed, agitation is being directed to make insurance against third party risks compulsory. This may seem an attempt to interfere with the liberty of the individual, and forensic arguments may be raised for and against it, but if one has suffered injury at the expense of another motor-cycle, and finds that the driver of the machine is unable to meet liability (assuming a court finds him culpable), the matter takes on a new aspect. It does seem unfair that one at present may be injured by traffic and may be unable to obtain compensation.

It certainly, then, seems sensible to insure against third-party risks and against personal injury; but as so many insurance companies issue " all-in " policies for a few shillings a year extra, it hardly seems worth while to differentiate, but to cover all risks. In every case the policy should be read through carefully, particularly clauses dealing with partial loss. For general guidance it is here stated that the premium should be less if the owner is the driver, if the vehicle is not used for public purposes, and if the insured party assumes liability of part of the loss up to a specified maximum, *which figure should be incorporated in the policy.* Also, if one has been insured for, say, two years, without claiming on the company, the subsequent subscription should be reduced. These rules, it is repeated, are not absolute—different companies may vary in details—but in any case they are fair points and useful ones on which to bargain. Insist on a " No Claim " Rebate Clause, which means that in the event of no claim being made over a stated period, a percentage of the premium is refunded.

CHAPTER III

DRIVING

WE will assume that the reader has registered his machine, obtained his driving licence, and complied with all the other necessary preliminaries. He will now be anxious to get the machine on the road.

PREPARING FOR A RUN

It is worth while giving a few minutes, thought and experiment to the subject, before actually sallying forth.

Place the machine on the stand by releasing the latter from its clip by a smart downward tap with the toe, placing the foot against it as it rests on the ground and pulling the machine back by means of the back fork stays. Do *not* pull it back by means of the saddle, for you may, in the course of time, break a saddle spring by such practice. Now remove the filler cap nearest the saddle, and fill the petrol tank. A large funnel fitted with a fine gauze should be used so as to prevent foreign matter entering the tank. Fill up the oil compartment, which is situated in the fore part of the tank (special cylinder oil is obtainable for the purpose). Remove the filler cap from the right-hand end of the gear box, and insert the specially prepared cylinder oil, until it comes level with the lip of the filler spout and no more can be poured in. Then replace the cap and tighten up with a spanner.

Lubricating the Engine. This is one of the most important points to be remembered in managing a motor-cycle. Whilst it is true that the engine will not run until it has a supply of petrol, it is equally true that it will not run *very long* unless it is kept well supplied with lubricating oil. The friction of the different parts would cause some of the softer metals employed in the bearings to get hot and expand beyond the working point, and the engine would stop suddenly with the bearings or the connecting rod damaged. This is what is technically known as " seizing up." The first thing to do is to open the needle valve of the sight feed (which is the knurled knob having the figures 1, 2, 3, 4, marked round it and situated on the front left-hand side of the tank (Fig. 36), see also page 23) of the lubricating system (fully explained on page 53 and illustrated on page 55) a few turns, and push down the pump plunger smartly until it

DRIVING

remains down. The barrel is then charged and oil flows through the sight feed. When the plunger rises to the top the pump is empty. Repeat this operation three or four times. The engine will then be sufficiently charged for starting, and the drip may be set at the desired flow by adjustment of the valve. Make certain that the oil tap is " on " (with the 2·49 h.p. models a tap is not fitted).

Petrol Supply to the Engine. The next thing to do is to turn on the petrol by turning the lever to the position marked ON. When a priming tap is fitted (it is not fitted to all models) the tap is off when it is pointing vertically downwards. If moved upwards towards the front, it allows the petrol to flow along the priming tube; while if moved upwards towards the back, it turns the petrol on to the carburettor as explained above.

The Various Controls and Their Purpose. The handlebar controls may be likened to delicate nerves which convey messages from the hands of the driver to the inside of the engine. They afford a striking example of the saying " Knowledge is power." The driver who knows the function of each control is able to make the engine do as he pleases, within reasonable limits, whilst the man who has not bothered to find out the exact purpose of each lever, may possibly be unable to start or stop the engine at will, and will almost certainly be unable to get the engine to run economically. The three main controls to the engine are (1) the gas supply, (2) the air supply, (3) the spark control for advancing and retarding the spark. There are also one or two minor controls, such as the exhaust lifter, which is used chiefly for starting, and the decompressor, which has a similar function. These are described in detail later. Another most important control is the clutch. This is simply a device for disconnecting the engine from the gear box at will, so that the engine can run without causing any movement of the machine. The gears are controlled by the gear lever, which will be found on the right-hand side of the tank. Anyone who has ridden a three-speed-gear bicycle will know why gears are necessary. The low gear is to make matters easier for the engine when the machine is travelling up a steep hill. The second gear is for easing matters on a hill which does not tax the engine to its utmost. The top gear is for normal travelling on the level or up slight inclines and also for travelling down hill. We shall have more to say about the intelligent use of the speeds a little later.

Operating the Controls for Starting the Engine. Open the throttle lever, which is the lower of the two control levers on the right handlebar, a distance equal to about one-third of its full movement. In this position it will be roughly parallel to the handlebar, as the levers open from left to right. Leave the air lever shut, that is as far to the left as it will go. This is the upper and shorter of the two levers. The lever above the left handlebar is the spark advance lever. Moving it from left to right advances the spark. Set this at about two-thirds advance, that is two-thirds of its total travel from its extreme left-hand position. Now pull up the little decompressor lever on the right-hand side of the engine as far as it will go (a decompressor is not fitted to the 2·49, 3·49, 7·70 and 9·86 models, and in these cases the machine should be started by operating the exhaust-valve lifter which in the 2·49 models is operated by a lever incorporated in the magnets control). See that the gear lever on the right-hand side of the machine is in the neutral position. If the lever should happen to be in another position, raise the exhaust-valve lifter (fitted to the left handlebar), revolve the engine by means of the kick starter, and at the same time push the gear lever into the neutral position. Never attempt to move the gear lever while the engine is stationary.

Starting the Engine. Everything is now ready for starting the engine, and all that it is necessary to do is to push down the kick-starter pedal smartly with the foot (of course using the exhaust valve lever for a portion of the kick-starter stroke), when the engine should fire at once. Provided the instructions given above as to the setting of the various levers have been carefully followed, the engine should start at the first or second depression of the kick starter.

Priming the Engine. If the engine feels very stiff when the kick starter is depressed, it may be advisable to prime the cylinder by opening the cock on top of the cylinder, and allowing a few drops of petrol to run into it by turning the petrol tap forwards as explained above. This will free the piston and make it more easy to operate the kick starter. Be careful not to put too much petrol into the cylinder when priming, and never prime at all unless it is really necessary.

Procedure after Engine has Started. As soon as the engine starts, push down the decompressor lever with the foot and open the air lever until a proper mixture is obtained, and the engine is firing regularly. It should be noted that the positions given above for the air, throttle, and spark levers are only approximate. A rider can only ascertain by experience the lever positions which enable him to start his own machine most easily. The "sound" and "feel" of a machine which will tell the rider that the engine is running well cannot be imparted by printed instructions.

The Action of the Controls. Let the engine run for a minute or two on the stand, but do not race it. Meanwhile note the results obtained by opening and shutting the throttle and air levers, advancing and retarding the spark, and operating the exhaust valve lifter, so as to become familiar with their operation.

Operating the Clutch and Gears. With the machine still on the stand and the engine still running, sit on the saddle and practise operating the clutch and gears. Raise the clutch lever on the outside of the left handlebar, and push the gear lever on the right from the neutral into the low gear position, then allow the clutch to engage by gently releasing the lever with the left hand. The back wheel will gradually speed up, and by the time the lever has been fully lowered, the wheel will be revolving steadily. To change the gear, move the gear lever smartly into the desired position. The clutch should be disengaged whilst the change is being made so as to reduce the shock to the machine as much as possible. Ten minutes spent becoming familiar with the method of gear changing, declutching, advancing and retarding the spark, will be well worth while. Once on the road, especially if there is much traffic about, the novice will find it rather difficult to think of all these small items. After a little practice their use will become second nature, but it is highly desirable to make their first acquaintance in the calm security of the cycle shed or garage. If the reader has ridden an ordinary push bicycle he will find no difficulty in balancing the motor cycle, and, if anything, the balance will be found to be decidedly easier.

THE FIRST SPIN

Now, standing on the left-hand side of the machine, push it gently off the stand, and swing the latter up into position. Now mount the machine, the engine being still running, raise the clutch lever (on outside of left handlebar) to its fullest extent, and push the gear lever into *low gear position*. Then engage the clutch by gently and slowly releasing the clutch lever with the left hand at the same time gradually opening the throttle, and the machine will start away smoothly and gather speed. Be careful always to disengage the clutch fully before moving the gear lever from the neutral position. Of course, when the rider is used to the machine, or if the machine has a sidecar, it is not necessary to put it on the stand to start it. The kick-starter can easily be operated by the rider when seated on the saddle.

Changing Gear. As soon as the machine is well under way, change to second gear. If a three-speed model, next accelerate to about 20 miles per hour, and then change to top gear. Always declutch when changing gear, and having made the change let the clutch in again slowly. When reducing speed, whether because the machine is climbing a steep hill or for any other cause, never let the engine labour on top gear. As soon as the engine seems inclined to labour change down into second gear. This is done merely by pushing the gear lever forward into the desired position. A similar operation enables the rider to change from second to low gear, if the speed similarly becomes too low for the second gear. Do not be afraid to change to a lower gear if it is thought desirable. The gear box is on the machine for use, and far more harm is done by letting the engine labour and thump unnecessarily on a high gear than by letting it " rev " a little on a lower gear. If very slow running is desired, as for instance when negotiating dense traffic, change into bottom gear and partly disengage the clutch. The clutch is fitted with special friction linings, and cannot be damaged by a reasonable amount of slipping when slow running is required.

The Exhaust-Valve Lifter. Do not control the speed of the engine by operating the exhaust-valve lifter. The speed should always be controlled by the throttle lever, for reasons explained presently, and the exhaust lifter should only be used for starting purposes.

Coasting. When descending hills the clutch may be disengaged and the engine stopped altogether, so that the machine coasts down like a bicycle. After coasting down a hill do not attempt to start the engine by means of the clutch if the low gear is engaged or serious damage may result. Release the clutch and engage high gear, open the throttle slightly, and let the clutch in gradually until the engine starts.

Acceleration. It is always wise when driving to avoid violent acceleration, because wheel-spin as well as skids are likely to occur, with decidedly bad effects on the tyres. Always endeavour to take up slowly and evenly, and to accelerate gradually. Whenever possible, regulate the speed by opening or closing the throttle gradually, not suddenly, and use so much air that the engine can be felt to be running under its best conditions. Do not run the engine with the air lever nearly closed for any length of time, otherwise the engine overheats.

DRIVING

Lubrication Details. Watch the drip feed occasionally to see if the lubrication system is working properly. A suitable setting for average running is about six notches or half a turn of the adjusting valve. Over lubrication will at once be apparent by the undue amount of smoke from the exhaust. If so, reduce the rate of drip, but always bear in mind that it is better to over lubricate than give insufficient oil. Particularly is this so with regard to a new engine. If sufficient oil is not obtained through the mechanical pump, this should be supplemented occasionally by the hand pump.

For high speed work, an extra two notches or so may be given. At the commencement of a ride, give a charge of oil from the hand pump to ensure that there is a sufficiency of oil in the crank-case. The oil is fed by gravity from the tank to the small pump, which consists of a worm operating in a tight sleeve in the timing gear cover, and the tap on the right-hand side of the tank should be turned on, i.e. downwards, the whole of the time the engine is running. The pump forces the oil along a second pipe to the sight feed on the near side of the machine, and in turn the lubricant flows to the engine by way of the third pipe, the lower end of which is attached to the flexible rubber connection of the crank-case.

The auxiliary pump which is attached to the sight feed is for the purpose of assisting the lubrication, and should only be used when the engine is put under particular stress, such as when climbing a fairly steep hill, or being driven at high speeds. The pump cannot, of course, be operated until the plunger is released by moving back the catch fitted to the gland nut, and the use of the auxiliary pump will in no way interfere with the working of the mechanical pump.

The Advance and Retard. Drive with the spark in the position in which the machine accelerates best. A retarded spark causes overheating and excessive petrol consumption.

How to Stop. Having told the reader how to start and ride the machine, it is imperative that he should know how to stop it. The sequence for stopping is as follows : (1) Close throttle ; (2) raise clutch lever ; (3) apply foot-brake gradually as found necessary.

Use of the Brakes. What has been said about violent acceleration applies with equal force to the other extreme—violent braking, or deceleration. One of the most frequent causes of skidding is sudden application of the brakes, due to the locking of the wheel. It is this sudden locking which causes a skid, but whether a skid takes place or not, the effect on the tyres is bad.

Adjusting the Brakes. Occasionally it is necessary to adjust the brakes, to compensate for wear. The adjustment should be such that the brake is not rubbing the drum when in the " off " position, or power will be lost in overcoming this extra friction. This can be done by placing the machine on the stand, with the gear lever in neutral, and spinning the back wheel. The same process holds true if a front brake is fitted. Nor should the adjustment necessitate a comparatively large movement of the pedal before the brake comes into operation. The cables operating the front brake need attention every now and then, for they are liable to become frayed. Don't forget to smear the brake springs with vaseline, and to coarsen the surfaces of the fibre shoes when they become glazed through constant use, but be careful to keep the vaseline off the brake shoes.

Oil on the Brakes. The reader is warned not to let oil drip on to the brake drums or surfaces, or when the brake is wanted in an emergency it will slip until the oil is squeezed or burnt out.

Methods of Stopping Without Using the Brakes. Leaving out involuntary stops, the other possible method is by raising the exhaust lever. (Magneto cut outs are not fitted to B.S.A. machines.) A good driver uses his brakes as little as possible. The methods given in the last paragraph won't stop the machine suddenly, but the reader is recommended to cultivate the habit of always allowing plenty of space in which to pull up.

Jab Braking. It should be remembered that if the roads are greasy, it is almost an impossibility to pull up suddenly without experiencing skidding. Special care should, therefore, be exercised when driving under these conditions, and the speed of the machine should be reduced when approaching cross roads. The brake should be applied by jabbing, and not with a steady pressure. This prevents the wheel from becoming locked in one position. The jabs should be steadily, not suddenly, applied.

CONCERNING THE TYRES

The pressure to which the tyres are inflated has an important bearing on the questions of comfort, tyre life, braking efficiency, and life of the machine.

" Hard " Tyres. A tyre inflated too hard does not absorb its share of the road shocks set up by potholes, etc., but passes them on to the springs of the front forks. The rider also will be jolted unnecessarily.

"**Soft**" **Tyres.** Dealing with the opposite extreme, tyres inflated to too low a pressure soon wear out, because part of the wear is taken by the "wall," or side, of the tyre, which is not meant to come into contact with the road at all. A "soft" tyre may be comfortable from the rider's point of view, but it may allow the rim to come into contact with the road and cause dents.

The Correct Tyre Pressure. The tyres should be inflated so that when the rider is seated on the saddle they slightly bulge where they meet the road. As there is more weight on the back wheel than on the front, obviously the front wheel will not need to be inflated quite so hard as the rear to effect the same degree of bulge.

Sidecar Alignment and its Effect on Tyres and Steering. Sidecar alignment, if defective, has a bad effect on the tyres and steering, causing the tread to wear on one side. If the tyre is noted to be wearing in this manner, remedy the sidecar alignment and reverse the cover, so that the tyre wear is equalized. See also page 73.

DRIVING A COMBINATION

The actual driving and engine control of a combination does not differ from a solo machine, and the instructions already given need not be repeated here. A solo machine rider will experience a little strangeness with a sidecar outfit, due to the offset drag of the sidecar, which tends to make steering difficult at first by continually edging the machine to the left side of the road and to draw the machine to one side. It is good practice to obtain confidence by taking the machine to the top of a hill and coasting down with free engine, with the foot ready to operate the brake in case of emergency. The assistance of a friend who may own a sidecar outfit is of inestimable value, for he may be induced to drive the machine whilst the owner rides in the sidecar and receives instructions. The driver in this case should explain his every action, and after a time should change places with the owner, directing the latter from the sidecar. If, however, the help of an experienced driver of a combination cannot be obtained, the assistance of a friend who is willing to occupy the sidecar should be obtained, for it is risky to endeavour to learn to drive a sidecar outfit without a passenger or even ballast of some sort to keep the sidecar down. Even an experienced rider dislikes driving a machine with an empty sidecar, for it has a tendency to bounce and lift when making a turn.

Making a Left-hand Turn with a Combination. Left-hand turns with a combination should always be taken extremely cautiously, because owing to the offset points of support (two wheels on one track and only one on the other), centrifugal force tends to overturn the machine. There is no need to explain the mechanics of this fact. It is sufficient to say that the tendency is there, and that left-hand turns should be taken more slowly than right-hand turns. The sidecar passenger on very sharp left-hand turns should lean outwards, away from the driver, as this lessens the tendency of the machine to overturn.

PILLION RIDING

The pillion rider must sit as closely as possible to the driver, and also as " easily " or limply as possible. Special foot-rests may be obtained ready for fitting to the machine. Ladies should sit facing the near side, with their feet hanging loose and not resting on the backstays nor stuck out. The passenger should sit still, and not lean in either direction, even when rounding corners. Although the machine itself will be " banked," or inclined, when going round a corner, the passenger should endeavour to keep his or her body in the same relation to the machine as when riding on a straight stretch of road. A pillion rider, if sitting astride, can often help to maintain the balance of the machine in traffic, or when taking corners at a low speed, by resting his feet very lightly on the ground.

PROCEDURE ON HILLS

Stopping on Hills. A solo machine should always be left with the front wheel pointing *up* the hill, as in this position it cannot " lift " from its stand of its own accord. A combination should also be left in a similar manner, one of the wheels being jammed against the kerbstone or bank and the front wheel turned towards the kerb so that any movement tends to jam the wheel still harder. The low gear should also be engaged.

Starting on Hills. With regard to starting on hills, if the latter are of lesser gradient than one in seven, no difficulty should be encountered if the methods already outlined are adopted. If the hill is steeper, adopt the following procedure : Lift the clutch and apply the brake, the latter operation preventing the machine from running downhill. With the brake on, start the engine, race it a little, and with low gear engaged gradually release the brake, *at the same time gradually letting in the clutch*. This dual action requires practice in order to be carried out effectively,

DRIVING

and the beginner may have to start his engine four or five times until he has acquired the knack.

Starting Downhill. Undoubtedly the best method of starting downhill is to coast down with the clutch disengaged and top gear engaged, until the machine has gathered a fair speed, when the clutch should be slowly engaged.

Braking on Hills. In descending steep hills of appreciable length when the brake would be on for some seconds, use the front and rear brakes alternately, for this prevents the parts of the brake getting very hot.

Using the Engine as a Brake. When descending very steep hills connect low gear at the *top of the hill*, and allow the machine to run down with the throttle closed. On a new machine the novice will probably be astonished at the very powerful braking action this produces. Care must be taken to open the throttle before reaching the bottom of the hill, as otherwise the machine may lose way and pull up unexpectedly. It is not considered good practice to open the exhaust valve when using the engine in this way. The sudden local cooling of certain portions of the engine is liable to cause strains in the material of the cylinder.

RULES OF THE ROAD

After the first two or three spins the reader will find that he has acquired plenty of confidence in the machine, but a word of caution is necessary at this stage, as accidents frequently happen when the driver, in the flush of his newly-acquired control of the machine, feels inclined to throw caution to the wind, forgetting that he has not yet acquired the experience which is sometimes necessary to pull one through an emergency safely. The instructions on driving already given relate to the mechanical details of driving of the machine. The aspect which we must now consider is that concerned with driving as related to other traffic on the road, the rules and conventions of the road, and other matters not connected with the machine. So that the reader may gain experience without having to bother his head with these details, the first spin for preference should not take place in a busy thoroughfare; a quiet district should be selected, and practice obtained in slacking speed, and pulling up, closing and opening the throttle, changing gear, etc., so that these movements can be carried out semi-instinctively. As experience is gained, confidence grows, and one's fingers automatically do the right things unconsciously as occasion arises. Then comes the time

28   BOOK OF THE B.S.A.

when the reader is able to carry out longer journeys and cross country runs, perhaps to see friends with whom to enthuse over his newly-acquired treasure.

The Proper Side of the Road. A motorist normally should keep to the left-hand side of the road, except when overtaking another vehicle, when he must pass on the off or right side.

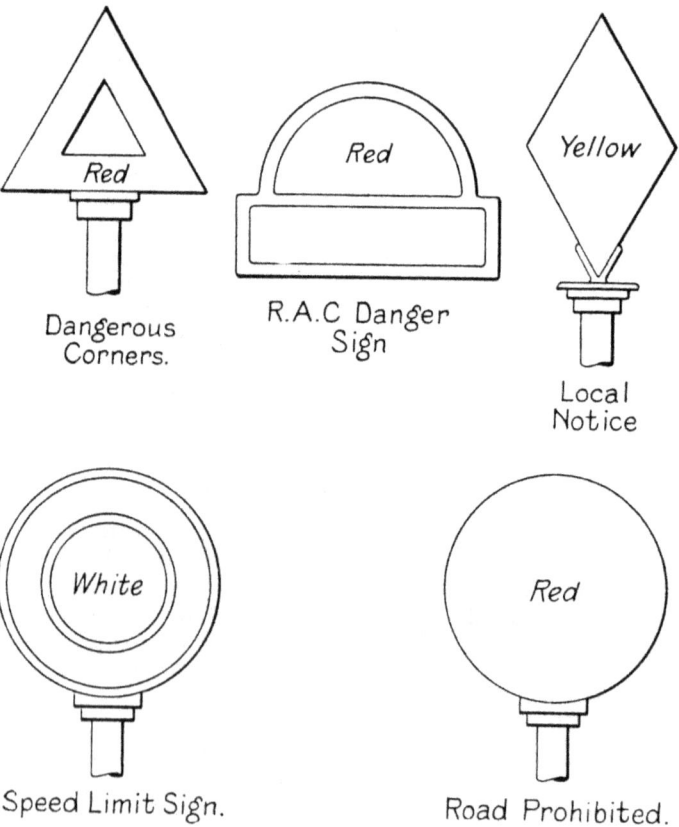

Fig. 17.—Conventional Road Signs

Road Signs. It is compulsory to observe road signs relating to traffic control. These are shown diagrammatically in Fig. 17, which explains itself.

Speed Limit. A speed limit of 20 miles per hour is the maximum speed on the highway where no other speed limit is fixed ; in

DRIVING

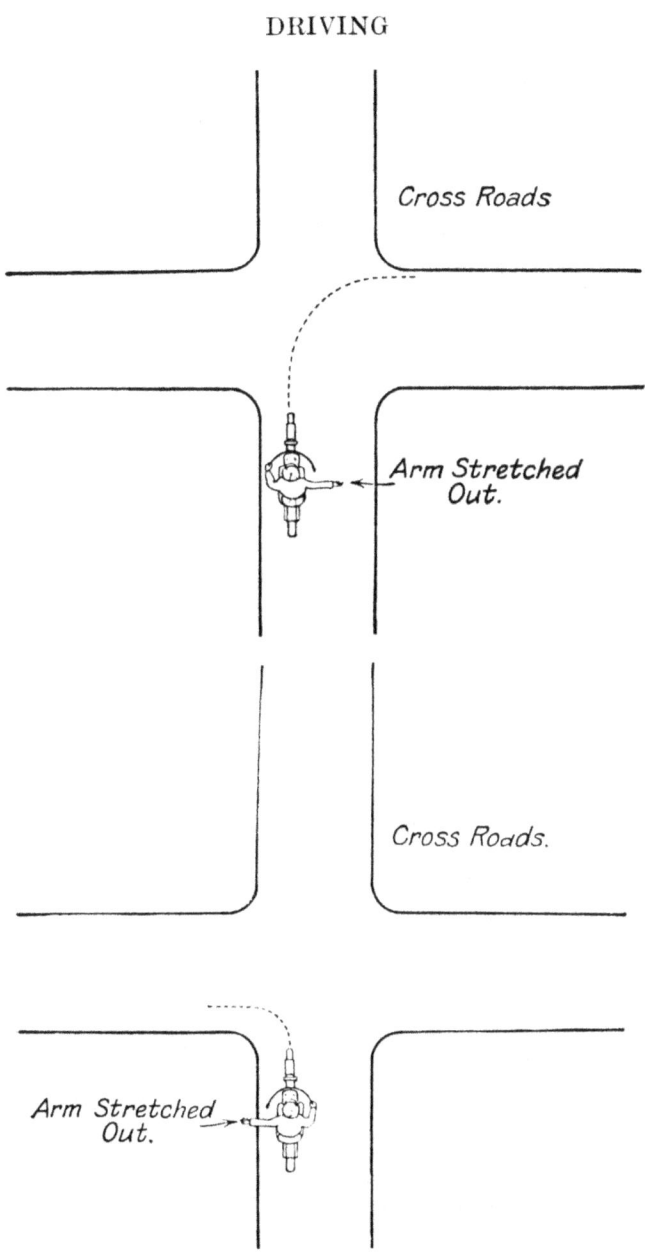

Fig. 18.—How to Warn Following Traffic that you are About to Turn to Left or Right

this respect it is worth pointing out that the offence " driving to the danger of the public," does not necessarily have relation to the speed of the vehicle. You can drive to the danger of the public at 3 m.p.h.

DRIVING IN TRAFFIC

The driving of a motor-cycle in traffic is a subject which really requires a book to itself, for the instances and conditions on which instruction could be given are multitudinous, and it would be impossible within the limits of this book to anticipate and deal with all of them. The more general conditions met with in traffic driving are, however, considered.

Cross Roads and Corners. Cross roads and corners, perhaps, present the greatest source of danger, and one should always anticipate the presence of a badly-driven vehicle, and pass or negotiate corners at slow speed. When making a turn either to the right or to the left, adopt the scheme shown in Fig. 18, which apprises approaching as well as following traffic of your intentions. The dotted lines indicate the direction that should be taken.

How to Take a Corner. After the beginner has successfully negotiated several " straight " runs, he may be excused for feeling a little nervous when he comes to turn a corner, but there is really very little in it. Many expert riders prefer to lean the cycle inward on a curve, and to lean the body in the opposite direction. This is probably the most satisfactory method, but it requires a little practice. The other method is to lean both the cycle and the body inwards.

Stopping in Traffic. To stop in traffic, go into low gear, declutch, and use the back brake alone, putting the latter only half on for a second or so and then, when the machine is considerably slowed down, putting it on full.

There is no need to stop the engine as some in emergency may be tempted to do, unless the stoppage is likely to be a lengthy one. Keep the clutch disengaged and throttle the engine down until it " ticks " over. If the stoppage is of more than three or four minutes duration, it may be advisable to stop it to prevent it getting overheated.

As a general rule, reserve the front brake for extreme emergencies, when it should be applied at the same time as the back brake.

Warning that you are about to stop should be given as in Fig. 19, and in this respect it is important to remember that the

DRIVING

stop should not be too sudden; you must allow the driver of the vehicle behind you time to interpret your intentions and to pull up, otherwise he may run into your back wheel.

Pottering in Traffic. Sometimes the reader will find that he is compelled to ride in a stream of slow-moving traffic, and he should do this by engaging low gear and closing the throttle till the engine ticks over. Or he may throttle down and use the decompressor, with second gear engaged.

Passing other Traffic. Where the width of the road allows, always pass other vehicles as widely as possible.

Led Horses. A led horse should always be led on the wrong side of the road. It is advisable to give them as wide a berth as possible. They should be passed on the near side.

Passing Tramcars. Tramcars may be passed on either side, but if the offside is clear, it is wise to pass on that side, and that fact would go in one's favour in case of accident. Legally considered, the road is intended for traffic, and loitering, strictly speaking, is illegal.

FIG. 19.—WARNING FOLLOWING TRAFFIC THAT YOU ARE ABOUT TO STOP

Tramlines and Skids. Tramlines are dangerous at all times, but wet ones are extremely so. Therefore, if a skid is to be avoided, so should riding on the tramlines, especially if the machine is a solo. When crossing tramlines do so as near as possible at a right-angle. There is then little danger of a skid; but to cross them at a "flat" angle is to ask for trouble.

The same instruction holds good for the stone setts of the centre rail tram system, known as the "underground" system.

Traffic Blocks. When a block of traffic can be observed some distance ahead, slow down gradually. The practice sometimes indulged in of approaching it at speed, and suddenly applying the brakes is not altogether devoid of risk.

The Camber of the Road. Owing to the tendency of heavy vehicles to sideslip when driven on the near side of the road, the drivers of them prefer to drive on the crest. Although this may leave an equal space on either side, it is not advised to pass the vehicle on the wrong side, but to give warning of approach, so that the driver may draw in to enable his vehicle to be passed on the proper side.

Driving Behind a Tram. The short distance in which trams can pull up should be borne in mind when following one of these vehicles, and it is wise always to keep a reasonable distance behind.

Unattended Animals on the Road. Animals, such as horses, cows, pigs, sheep, etc., straying on the roadway represent a real danger, for they do the most stupid things, and when the reader may think an animal is about to leave the roadway and pass on to the grass, it will suddenly dash back into the middle of the road and make passing difficult. It is almost superfluous to tell the reader to stop in such a circumstance and to wait until the animal is well clear, or to drive it away. Do not endeavour to do this by shouting or vigorous operation of the horn; this may daze or infuriate the animal.

Modifying Traffic Rules. Safety is the main consideration, and the fact that another may be in the wrong necessitates, perhaps, modifications of the rules. Dogmatically adhering to the law will not save your life when it is endangered by another breaking it, and the doctrine of " doing a great right by doing a little wrong " cannot be altogether ignored. One may thus be compelled to drive the machine on to the footpath in order to avoid a collision.

The Importance of Looking Ahead. A keen look-out ahead avoids tight corners. One may observe over the top of a hedge a horse and cart about to turn into a road on the near side. This enables one to pull up at a safe distance, and the habit of taking a sweeping survey of the view ahead is one to cultivate, and in time becomes second nature. Give ample warning of approach by sounding the horn.

NIGHT RIDING

Almost all of the remarks already given apply to night riding. A red light ahead of course signifies a vehicle either stationary or going in the same direction, and procedure is obvious.

When meeting vehicles going in the opposite direction the glare from headlamps, particularly those of cars, is a source of danger, and although many vehicles are fitted with dimming devices, this practice is not invariable.

Generally speaking, one should drive at slower speed at night, and a keener look-out is necessary, especially when passing through lanes adjoining fields, owing to the possibility of straying animals.

Courtesy. The great point is to be courteous on the road and considerate to others, thus fostering the friendship and brotherhood of the open road. Bearing in mind the rules given, every road user is urged to consider the safety and comfort of others.

Remember always to—

Carry your driving licence.

Keep to the left of the road.

Go slow past schools and in populous places.

Overtake on the right, after seeing that the road in front is clear.

Give warnings with the right arm when slowing down or turning to the off-side.

Give way whenever possible to traffic approaching from the off-side.

Pass a led horse on its near side.

Conform to the lighting and registration regulations.

Recognize warning signs and speed restriction notices.

Realize the discomfort to others of dust and mud splashing.

When going down hill give way to traffic coming up.

Assist the police to regulate traffic by responding promptly to their signals.

Remember never to—

Cut in.

Overtake at cross roads, bends, in narrow village streets, or where an oncoming driver has the right of way.

Abuse the " audible warning of approach."

GENERAL REMARKS

By now the reader will probably be getting to know the sound of his engine. He will, no doubt, have noticed that when the throttle, air and spark are set " just right," the engine purrs along as steadily as can be desired. At other times it may be found that the running is not quite so regular, the engine may seem to thump unduly or there may be mystifying pops or misfires. Each motor-cycle engine has a personality of its own, and will only give of its best to a person who knows its peculiarities thoroughly. Your engine will try and let you know if you are not treating it properly, and if any unusual sound can be detected during running, the good driver will immediately look round to find the cause. He may find that his spark is too much retarded or too much advanced. He may find that his engine is receiving too much oil (shown by blue smoke coming out of the exhaust pipe), or too little oil, which can be detected by the sight feed lubricator and non-response of engine to throttle. The petrol supply may not be quite right, owing to a partially empty petrol tank or an air-lock in the petrol pipe, so that only driblets of petrol find their way to the carburetter, causing the supply to be intermittent, and resulting in mysterious misfires and stoppages. Again, it is possible for the float inside the carburettor to stick and allow the petrol to overflow. All these faults are dealt with in a later chapter dealing with faults and their remedies.

CHAPTER IV

HOW THE ENGINE WORKS

Elements of the Power Unit. There are three main portions of the power unit to be considered—the engine itself, the carburettor, which supplies the engine with the correct mixture of air and petrol gas, and the magneto, whose duty it is to supply a spark at the correct moment to ignite that mixture. These will now be considered.

Types of Engines. Let us deal with the engine first. There are two types into which all motor-cycle engines (and for that matter, motor-car engines) can broadly be classified—the two-stroke and the four-stroke, and in each type there are engines of one, two, or more cylinders. As, however, the number of cylinders does not affect the underlying principle (for an engine with more than one cylinder can be considered as a number of single-cylinder engines coupled together) the purpose of this chapter will be served if only single-cylinder engines are considered. Firstly then, regarding the four-stroke engine.

THE FOUR-STROKE ENGINE

Elements of the Four-stroke Engine. Fig 20 shows an ordinary single-cylinder motor-cycle engine as if it had been cut down the centre with a metal saw. It consists of the cylinder, crankcase (to which the cylinder is attached and which carries the bearings for the crankshaft), the piston, connecting rod (secured to the piston by means of the gudgeon-pin), the crankshaft (to which the connecting rod is also secured), the exhaust valve, inlet valve, induction pipe, and sparking plug. The piston is rendered gas-tight by means of piston rings. These rings are introduced to lessen the frictional area, because if the piston itself were made gas-tight in the cylinder, without any rings at all, the friction would be so great that a large amount of power would be lost in overcoming it. Connected to the induction pipe is the carburettor, which is connected by means of a pipe to the petrol tank, and driven from the crankshaft at half the speed of the latter is the magneto, which is connected by insulated wire to the sparking plug.

Principle of the Four-stroke Engine. It has been stated that the engine at present under consideration is known as a " four-stroke."

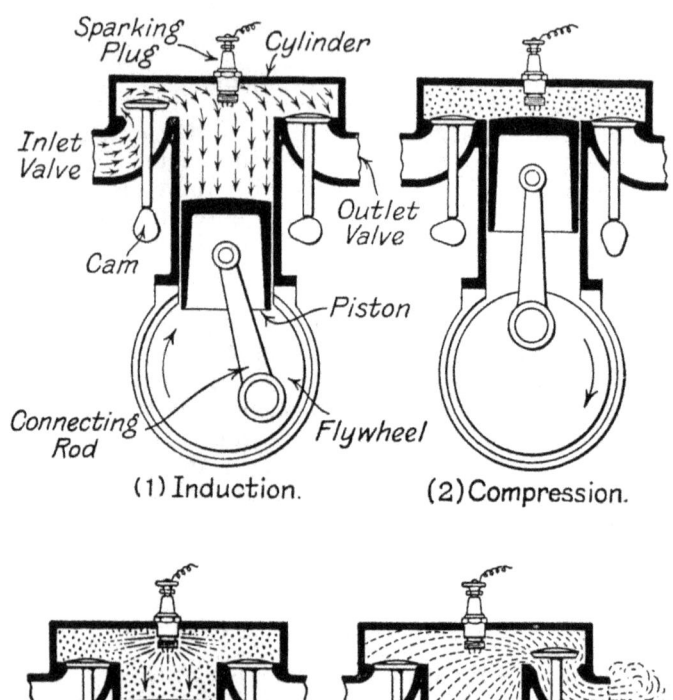
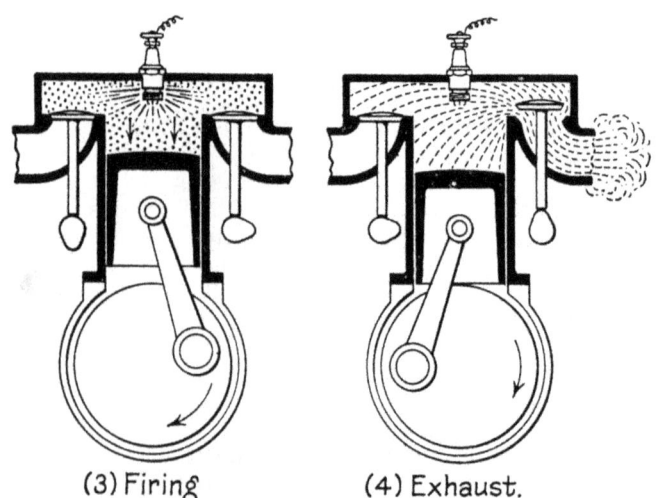

Fig. 20.—The Principle of the Four-Stroke Engine

HOW THE ENGINE WORKS

This is because there are four distinct strokes; firstly, the induction of the charge of petrol-and-air gas into the cylinder; secondly, the compression of that charge; thirdly, the explosion or ignition of it, and, fourthly, the exhausting of the burnt gases. The diagrams (Fig. 20) show the relative positions of piston and crank for these four strokes. Now, how is the charge of petrol gas introduced into the cylinder ? When the engine is caused to revolve, the piston exerts a powerful suction on the jet in the carburettor, and (1) the petrol is drawn through the induction pipe into the cylinder through the inlet valve, which is opened to allow the induced charge to pass into the cylinder by means of cams, which push on the valve stems. As soon as the piston reaches the bottom of its stroke, this valve is closed by means of the valve spring, and the piston (2), as it reverses its stroke and travels towards the top of the cylinder, compresses the charge of petrol which is trapped in it. Just before the piston reaches the top of its stroke, a spark occurs at the sparking plug point (only once every four piston strokes, be it noted) and (3) explodes the mixture, forcing the piston to the bottom of the stroke. As soon as it reaches this position, another set of cams operate the exhaust valve, which opens to allow the burnt charge to pass into the exhaust pipe, from whence it reaches the atmosphere after passing through a silencer embodied to reduce the noise.

The piston now commences to travel towards the top of the cylinder, but this time it does not compress the charge. This stroke is known as the exhaust stroke (4), because its purpose is thoroughly to scavenge the cylinder of the burnt gas. This is pushed out by the piston, and with this object in view the exhaust valve is arranged to remain open during the whole of this stroke, whilst the inlet valve remains closed. When the piston again reaches the top of its stroke, the exhaust valve closes, and the inlet valve commences to open, when the piston again sucks in a charge of petrol from the jet. And so this cycle of operations continues. It will be seen, then, how the four strokes of induction, compression, firing and exhaust operate.

The Function of the Flywheel. Were it not for the flywheel, the piston could not possibly return to the top of its stroke, and it is the purpose of the flywheel to store up sufficient power to keep the engine running during the strokes of exhaust, induction and compression.

THE PRINCIPLE OF THE CARBURETTOR

So much for the principles of the petrol engine; now with regard to the carburettor. This consists chiefly of what is known

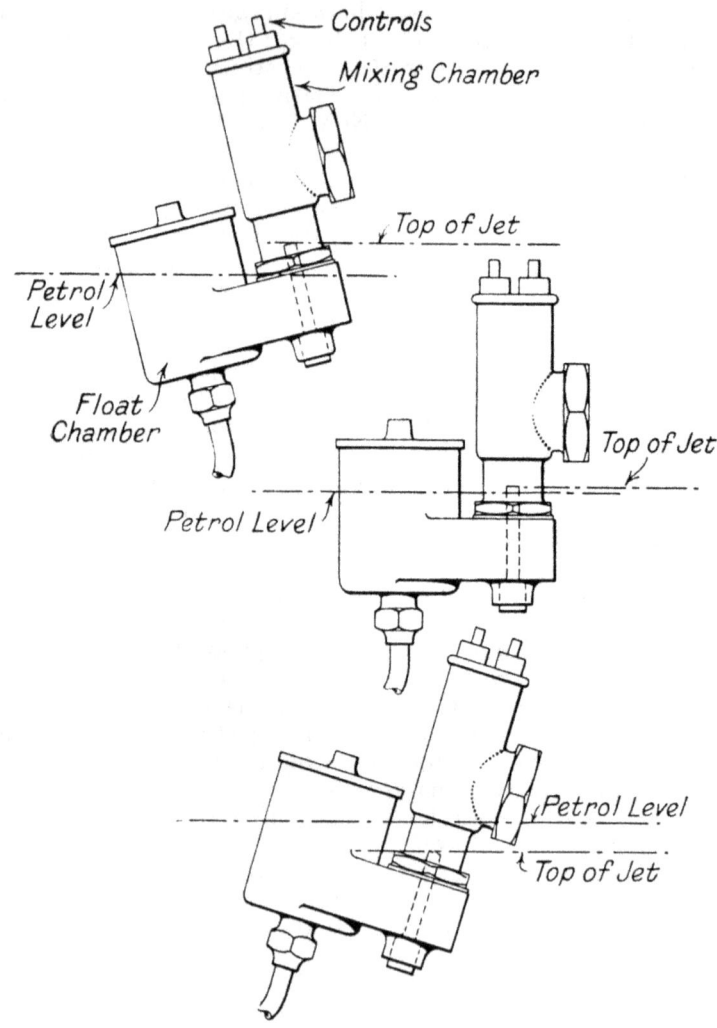

Fig. 21.—Diagram showing Relation between Petrol Level and Jet, and showing how Inclining the Machine Alters the Petrol Level

HOW THE ENGINE WORKS

as a float chamber, in which is a cork or metal float. Through the centre of this float, and fixed to it, is a needle with a tapered end, and as the petrol enters the float chamber this float rises (or "floats") like a float on a fishing line, until the petrol has reached the required level in the float chamber, when the tapered end of the needle fits close into a tapered hole in the base of the carburettor and cuts off the supply. This level is determined by the jet situated in close proximity to the induction pipe (see Fig. 21). The jet has a fine hole, through which the petrol is sucked by the engine. The choke tube of the carburettor usually contains two slides (the single-slide type is dealt with presently). The one nearest the jet is known as the throttle, and is operated by means of a lever fixed on the handlebars. The other slide, which is also controlled by means of a lever fixed to the handlebars, varies the area of the air intake and hence governs the velocity of the air. By closing the throttle the speed of the engine is reduced, and by closing the air the speed is also reduced. By varying the openings which these two slides control, the proportion of petrol to air introduced into the cylinder is varied.

THE MAGNETO

Present purposes are satisfied if it is stated that the magneto consists of two permanent magnets, and a coil wound upon an iron bobbin, known as the armature. This armature is caused to revolve (with the four-stroke engine) at half engine speed, by means of sprockets (one connected to the armature shaft and the other to the crankshaft) and a chain or by a train of gears, so that the spark caused by the coil becoming energized during the revolution of the armature occurs only once during two revolutions of the crank. It will thus be seen that this spark will occur at every four strokes of the piston, for reasons already explained.

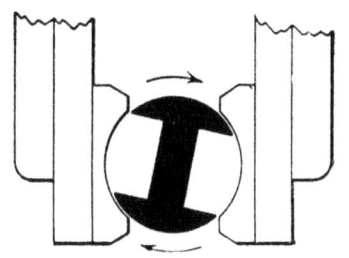

FIG. 22.—POSITION OF ARMATURE WHEN CONTACT POINT SHOULD START TO OPEN

Incorporated on the armature shaft is what is known as the make-and-break mechanism, as shown in the diagram (see Figs. 22 and 46), and, at the right moment, the cam carried on the cam-plate separates the two contact points, and causes a spark to occur at the plug points, thus firing the charge.

The Advance and Retard. Besides being able to control the speed of the engine by means of the carburettor slides, it may also be controlled by means of the advance and retard lever, which is fixed to the handlebars and causes the spark to occur about $\frac{1}{4}$ in. before top dead centre in the fully advanced, and about $\frac{1}{16}$ in. *after* top dead centre in the fully retarded position. Most engines have a " best " position for these levers, which can only be found by trial. (Refer also to page 20 of the chapter on Driving.)

CHAPTER V

MECHANICAL DETAILS OF THE B.S.A.

THE beginner is usually too enthusiastic and anxious to ride his machine to bother his head about its constructional details. Sufficient for him that the machine runs. There comes the time, however, when he begins to ponder over such matters, especially when overhaul becomes necessary, or when adjustment necessitates dismantling some part of the machine. A knowledge of the construction at such times is valuable, for it enables him to do the particular job much more quickly than he would if he had to fumble about to find out how the various parts were secured. Lack of such knowledge may easily be a direct cause of damage.

COMPONENTS OF THE MACHINE

When studying the machine it is easier to follow out the assembly if the parts are considered as units, and study should be directed to each unit as if the rest of the machine did not exist. The chief units are the wheels, the rear one of which is driven and enables the machine to " roll " or run along the road ; the frame, which carries the wheels and the motive power for driving them ; the engine (including the magneto, carburettor and tank) supplying the motive power ; the gear box and transmission, which enables the number of revolutions of the engine in relation to one revolution of the back wheel to be varied ; the lubrication system, whose duty it is to supply the engine with oil to prevent it from seizing or getting too hot ; the handlebars, by means of which the course of the machine is directed ; the front forks, which are sprung to absorb road shocks ; the saddle, and the sidecar. Whilst it would require a lengthy book to deal with all these items, it is felt that sufficient attention and instructions should be given to them here to enable the novice to understand them. Such knowledge makes for intelligent use and operation of the machine, for if the reader has a mental vision of, say, the gear box, he will know how to use it intelligently, and what *not* to do. Let us consider the details from the engine down to the wheels.

THE ENGINE

Parts of the Engine. We have already seen how the petrol engine works, and the elements of the engine (piston, crank, etc.)

were explained at the time. It may, then, fairly be supposed that the reader will not require further reference to this matter.

No detailed mention has yet been made of " side-valve " engine or " overhead-valve " engine.

The Side-Valve Engine. In the early forms of motor-cycles, what is known as superposed valves were used. That is to say, the inlet valve was placed immediately over the exhaust valve. The inlet valve usually was automatically operated by suction,

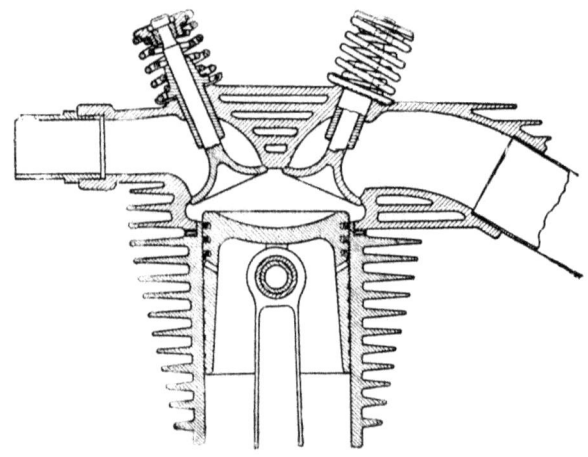

FIG. 23.—SECTION OF CYLINDER HEAD, 3·49 O.H.V. ENGINE

which caused it to lift on the induction stroke and admit the charge of petrol-and-air gas. Automatic valves, however, were so troublesome that mechanically-operated valves were introduced (the honour of introduction belongs to the Minerva Co.), and instead of the valves being superposed, they were placed side by side. It will be seen that the inlet valve, as well as the exhaust valve, is mechanically operated. By far the majority of cars and motor cycles now have this valve arrangement. Mechanically-operated superposed valves are in use to-day on several well-known makes of motor-cycles.

The Overhead-Valve Engine. Even as side-by-side valves were an improvement on superposed valves, so (theoretically, at any rate are overhead valves an improvement on side-by-side valves. The B.S.A. o.h.v. cylinder head is shown in Figs. 23 to 25. The advantages claimed for it are that a more perfect design of cylinder is possible, and that better carburation is obtainable as the turbulence (the swirling motion) of the gas, so necessary to efficient carburation, is not impaired. Two types of overhead-valve gear are in use to-day, one carried by a detachable cylinder head, and the other in a detachable seating. The wreckage which may result from the breakage of a valve where a

Fig. 24.—The 3·49 h.p. Overhead-Valve Cylinder Head

cage is not provided to prevent it dropping into the cylinder can easily be imagined. An engine fitted with overhead valves is more speedy than a similar model with side valves.

THE CUSH DRIVE

Purpose of the Cush Drive. The purpose of a cush (short for " cushion ") drive is to eliminate the harshness which accompanies the use of chain drive, and it certainly tends to reduce wear on the back tyre, and enables the power from the engine to be " picked up " gradually. With a belt-driven machine (or chain-and-belt) the cush drive is unnecessary, for the flexibility of the belt serves the same purpose as a cush drive. In actual practice the friction clutch itself is a cush drive, for it slips a little when " picking up." The positive dog clutch, of course, does not slip.

Fig. 25.—The 3·49 h.p. Overhead-Valve Engine, Valve—Gear Side

MECHANICAL DETAILS

New Pattern Cam-Cush Drive. In the newer models the above cush drive has been replaced by one of a different pattern, effecting the same purpose in another way. In this later pattern, one large coil spring connects the engine with the countershaft, the connection between the spring mounting and the engine shaft being in

FOR THE TECHNICAL READER

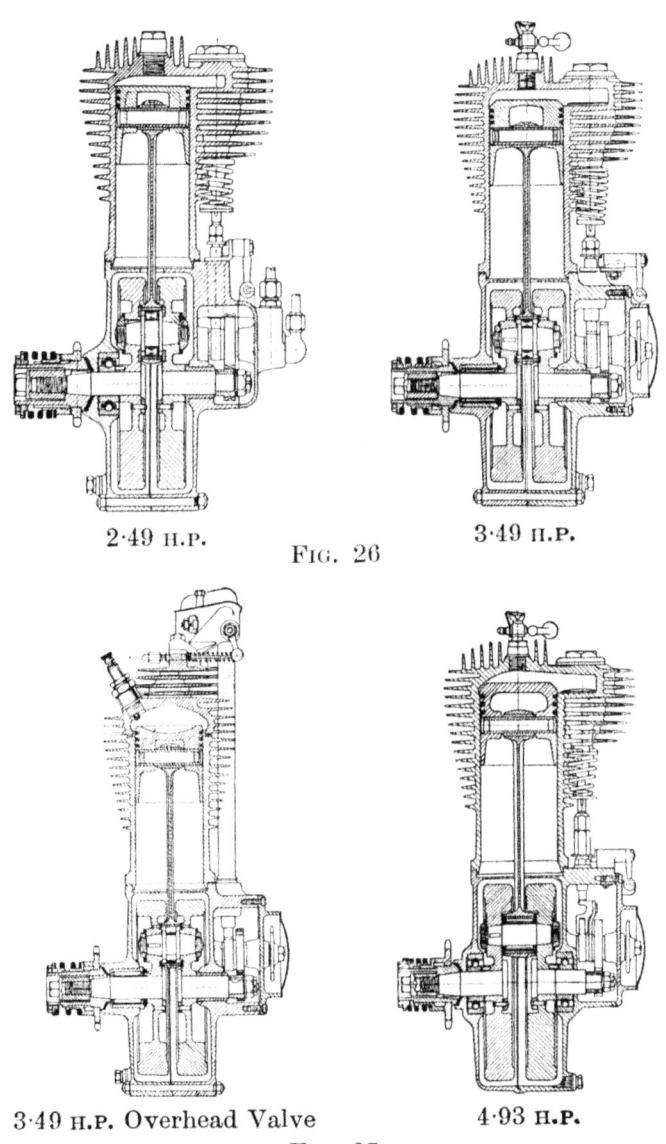

2·49 H.P.　　　　　　　3·49 H.P.
FIG. 26

3·49 H.P. Overhead Valve　　　4·93 H.P.
FIG. 27

FIGS. 26 & 27.—WHAT YOUR ENGINE LOOKS LIKE INSIDE

the form of a cam-faced serrated plate, but capable of a little give and take on either side. This is illustrated in Fig. 28.

The Two-Speed Countershaft Gear. In this gear box, as fitted to the 2·49 h.p. model, and shown by Figs. 30 and 31, gears are constantly in mesh, the change being effected by dogs. The

Fig. 28.—The Cam-Faced Cush Drive (with cover removed) as Fitted to 3·49 h.p. Side-Valve Model

gear-changing mechanism is enclosed within the box together with the kick-starter gear. The latter consists of the kick-starter crank connected to a quadrant which is mounted directly on the lay shaft. When operated, this meshes with a ratchet pinion mounted on the main shaft.

Change Speed Lever. The change speed lever is fitted direct to the gear box, and is provided with an outside selector quadrant, so that position of the gear lever can be readily seen. The clutch is left in to start the engine, the gear lever being in the neutral position.

The oil filler plug is fitted on the end plate, and the height is

MECHANICAL DETAILS OF THE B.S.A.

such that if the box is filled to this level, adequate lubrication is given to all moving parts.

The following are particulars of gear ratios for the 2·49 h.p. model, showing the ratio recommended. The 16-tooth sprocket on the engine shaft gives gears suitable for use in hilly country with heavy rider.

FIG. 29.—(Left) THE ALUMINIUM PISTON AND (Right) THE CAST IRON PISTON. NOTE THE GUDGEON-PIN FIXING

GEAR RATIOS FOR 2·49 H.P. MODEL

Sprocket Teeth on.			Gears.		
Engine Shaft.	Gear Box.	Rear Wheel.	High.	Low.	Model.
16	43 17	42	6·6	12·4	
17	43 17	42	6·2	11·7	Standard

GEAR RATIOS FOR THREE-SPEED 2·49 H.P. DE LUXE MODEL

Sprocket Teeth on.			Gears.			
Engine Shaft.	Gear Box.	Rear Wheel.	High.	Med.	Low.	Model.
16	43 17	42	6·6	9·8	14·5	
17	43 17	42	6·2	9·3	13·6	Standard

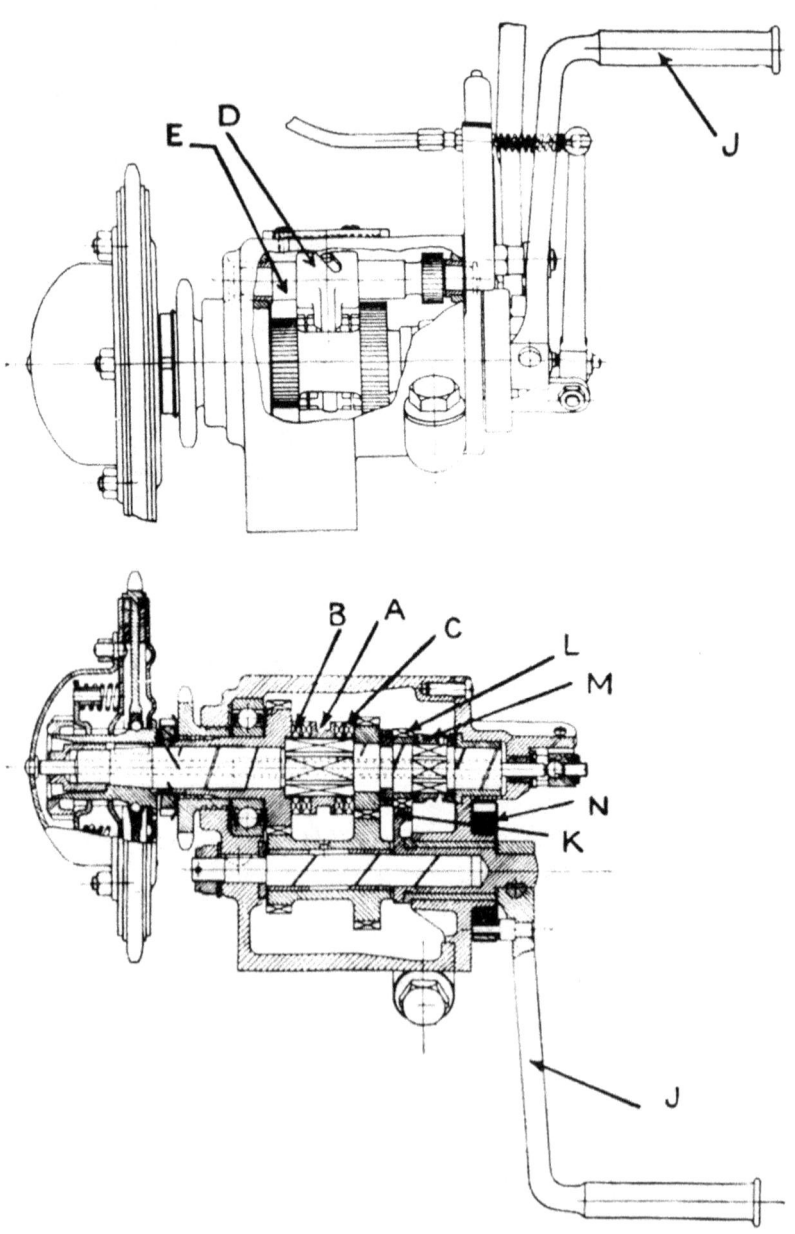

FIGS. 30 AND 31.—TWO-SPEED GEAR BOX
FITTED TO 2·49 H.P. MODELS

MECHANICAL DETAILS OF THE B.S.A.   49

The Three-Speed Countershaft Gear. This gear box, although similar in principle to that which is fitted to the heavier machines, is smaller and more compact. The three-speed gear box fitted to the 3·49 h.p. and the 4·93 h.p. models is, like the two-speed gear box, of the countershaft type, with all pinions in constant mesh, and an external clutch of the dry-plate variety.

The Dog Clutch. The changing of gears is effected by sliding dog clutches A and B (Fig. 33), and the method by which the dog clutches are given the necessary movement constitutes one of the principal features of the device. (See Figs. 30 to 33 for details of the two- and three-speed gear boxes.)

On the shaft C (Fig. 33), which is rotated by means of the pinion and quadrant D, which is operated by the lever at the side of the tank, are mounted two operating forks E and F, the arms of which engage in the grooves of the dog clutches A and B. Helical cam grooves are formed in these forks, which engage pegs G fixed in shaft C. When the shaft C is revolved by means of the operating mechanism, the pegs G cause the forks E and F to slide along, the cams being cut so as to give the required position to the sliding dog clutches, A and B.

The Low Gear. When the low gear is put into operation, the dog clutch B is moved into engagement with pinion J. The drive is transmitted by means of central shaft H and pinion I to pinion J, then through dog clutch B to shaft K and pinion L, which in turn drives pinion M, to which the rear chain sprocket N is attached.

The Second Gear. The second gear is obtained by rotating shaft C, which withdraws dog clutch B from engagement with pinion J into engagement with pinion T. The drive is then transmitted from shaft H through pinions O and T, then, as previously, through pinion L to pinion M and rear chain sprocket.

The High Gear. The high or normal gear is effected by a further rotating of shaft C, which withdraws dog clutch B from pinion T, and engages dog clutch A with pinion M, clutch B being retained in an inoperative position. Pinion sleeve M, with sprocket N is thus coupled direct to shaft H, pinions J, T and L revolving idly. When changing up from low to high gear it is imperative that the drive of the engine should be disengaged momentarily by releasing the clutch.

Engagement of Dog Clutches. A novel means of ensuring correct position of all gears is arranged in the gear box operating

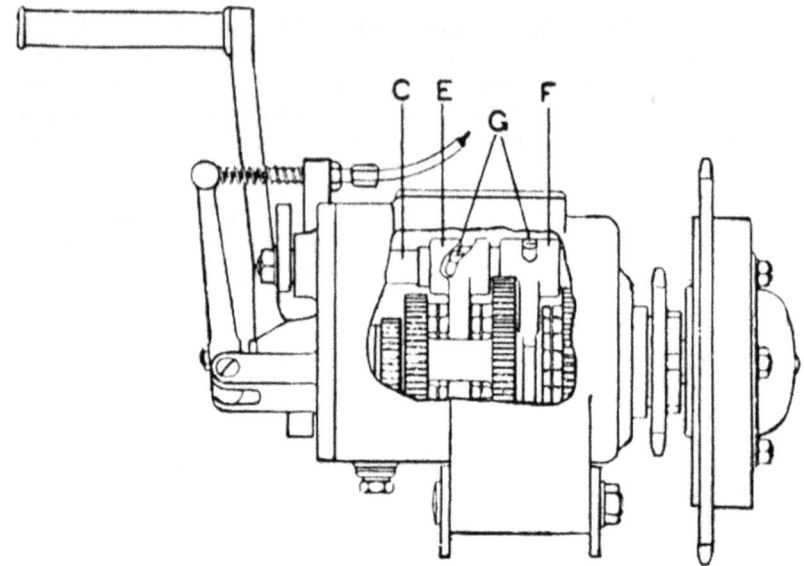

Fig. 32.—Three-speed Gear Box
(Outside View)

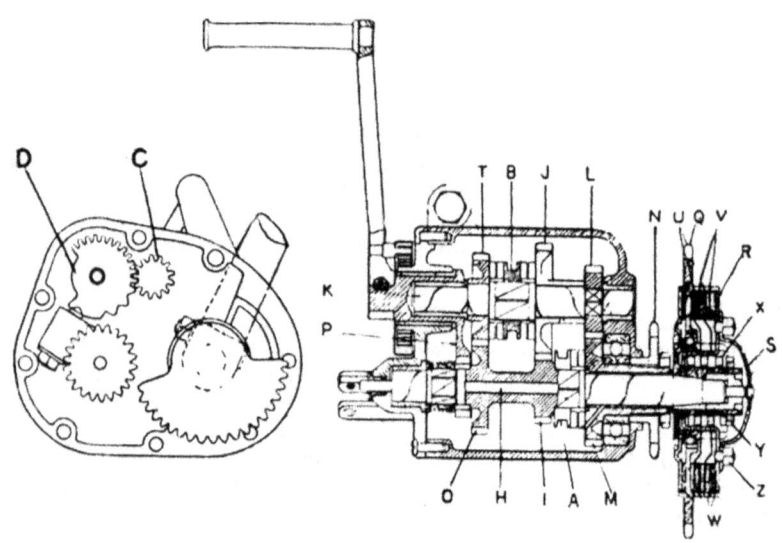

Fig. 33.—Three-speed Gear Box
(Inside View)

MECHANICAL DETAILS OF THE B.S.A.

mechanism. The quadrant D is formed with teeth round part of its circumference only. On the plain portion of the periphery a number of pockets are provided, which engage with a spring plunger mounted on the boss of the gear box cover. The spring plunger on change lever is thus dispensed with.

Starting the Engine. To start the engine, the gear lever is moved to the neutral position. Each dog clutch is now out of engagement. Movement of the kick-starter crank rotates quadrant P mounted on shaft K, which in turn engages with ratchet pinion mounted on shaft H. In order that its engagement shall be certain, without jamming, the first tooth in quadrant P is of special form. All difficulty of engagement is thus obviated. On the road, the engine can be started by means of the kick-starter only when the gear is in " neutral " position.

Position of Clutch When Starting. The clutch is left in to start the engine, the gear lever being in the neutral position. When the engine has been started, the clutch is withdrawn by a lever on the left of handlebar, and the low gear is then engaged by moving operating lever to the low gear position. The clutch can then be engaged, when it will be found that the load can be taken up in a particularly smooth and efficient manner.

General Procedure When Changing Gear. When changing gear this procedure should be followed: If the clutch is eased slightly when changing down from high gear to second, or second to low, the shock of engagement is reduced. Assuming high gear to be in operation, to change to second gear, the lever should be pushed forward smartly to the stop in the midway position, and to change to low gear, the lever should be moved slightly to the right to clear stop in gate, then being pushed smartly forward.

In the 2·49 h.p. model, low gear is the extreme rearward position of the gear lever.

The adjustment of the gear box is dealt with in Chapter VI.

As already stated, the three-speed gear box fitted to the 5·57, 7·70, and 9·86 h.p. models differs only in point of size and not in principle.

THE CLUTCH

The clutch is provided to enable the driver to " disconnect " the engine from the gear box when desired, and to enable the power from the engine to be gradually taken up. The half-tone

3·49 H.P. STANDARD MODEL

Sprocket Teeth On			Gears			Model
Engine Shaft	Gear Box	Rear Wheel	High	Middle	Low	
16	35	15	42	6·1	8·3	14·5	Comb.
17	35	15	42	5·8	7·9	13·6	Solo
18	35	15	42	5·4	7·4	12·9	
19	35	15	42	5·1	7·0	12·2	

GEAR RATIOS FOR 3·49 H.P. O.H.V. AND 4·93 H.P. MODELS

Teeth on Sprocket			Ratios			Model
¼″ Pitch		⅝″ Pitch				
Engine Shaft	Gear Box	Rear Wheel	High	Middle	Low	
21	43	15	42	5·7	7·8	13·5	Combination 3·49 and 4·93 h.p.
22	43	15	42	5·4	7·4	12·9	3·49 h.p. Solo
23	43	15	42	5·2	7·1	12·3	
24	43	15	42	5·0	6·8	11·8	4·93 h.p. Solo

5·57 H.P. MODEL

Sprocket Teeth On			Gears			Model
Engine Shaft	Gear Box	Rear Wheel	High	Middle	Low	
15	38	15	35	5·9	9·4	15	De Luxe Combination
16	38	15	35	5·5	8·8	14	Light Combination
17	38	15	35	5·2	8·3	13·3	Solo
18	38	15	35	4·9	7·8	12·5	

7·70 H.P. AND 9·86 H.P. TWIN MODELS

Sprocket Teeth On			Gears			Model
Engine Shaft	Gear Box	Rear Wheel	High	Middle	Low	
16	38	15	35	5·5	8·8	14	
17	38	15	35	5·2	8·3	13·3	De Luxe 7·70 h.p. Combination
18	38	15	35	4·9	7·8	12·5	{ Light 7·70 h.p. Combination { 9·86 h.p. Combination
20	38	15	35	4·4	7·14	11·4	7·70 h.p. and 9·86 h.p. Solo

(Fig. 34) in conjunction with the details given in the paragraph on the countershaft gear, makes explanation unnecessary.

Note the order in which the plates *U*, *V* and *W* are arranged, so that they can be assembled in the same order.

Fig. 34.—The B.S.A. Plate Clutch

THE DECOMPRESSOR

This is a device for facilitating easy starting, and it also allows the machine to be driven slowly, although this practice is not recommended. The decompressor is shown in Fig. 35. It permits a small percentage of the petrol gas sucked into the cylinder to be forced out during the compression stroke. The decompressor is so designed that on the compression stroke the exhaust valve is raised for a moment, so allowing some of the gas to escape and consequently reducing the compression pressure. It will thus be seen how the decompressor facilitates easy starting, and how, when the engine is running, slow running is obtained. A decompressor is not required on machines under 4 h.p., for their lower cubic capacity enables them to be run very slowly without chain snatch by throttle control only.

The B.S.A. decompressor is mechanically operated, a small cam lifting the valve mechanically.

THE LUBRICATION SYSTEM

As previously alluded to in an earlier chapter, this works on the principle of gravity feed from the tank to the small pump which consists of a worm operating in a tight sleeve in the timing gear cover. The pump forces the oil along a second pipe to the sight feed on the near side of the machine, and the oil flows to the engine by way of the third pipe, the lower end of which is attached to the flexible rubber connection of the crankcase.

The auxiliary hand pump which is attached to the sight feed is for the purpose of assisting lubrication, and is only intended for

Fig. 35.—Detail View of 3·49 h.p. Cylinder, Showing Exhaust Valve Lifter

use when the engine is under heavy load. For details of its use see the paragraph on lubrication (page 18) details in the chapter on driving.

The lubrication system is shown diagrammatically in Fig. 36.

LUBRICATION.

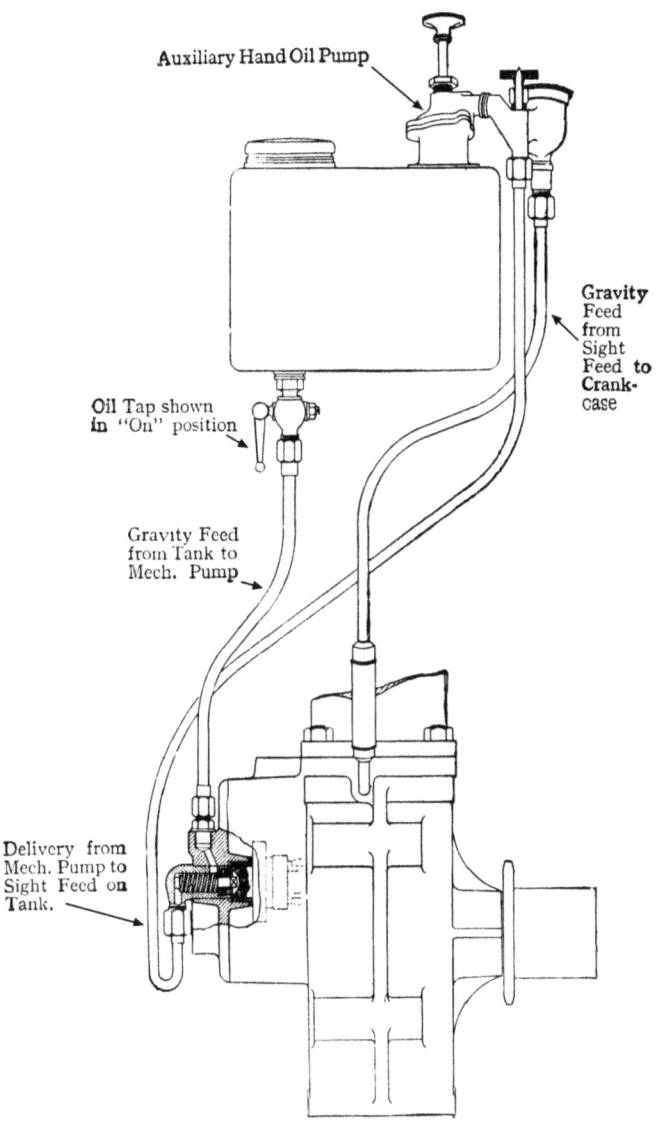

Fig. 36.—The Engine Lubricating System of the B.S.A.

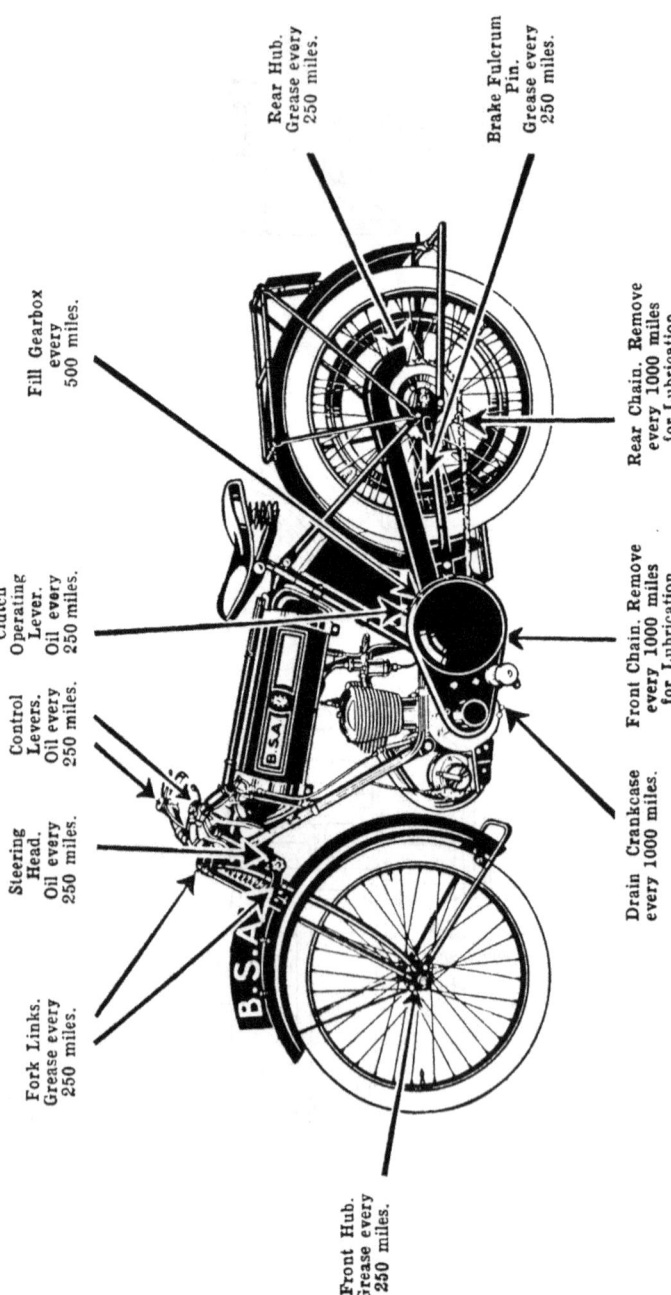

Fig. 37.—The Important Parts Requiring Lubrication

THE CARBURETTOR

A sectional view of the carburettor usually fitted to B.S.A. mounts (the Amac) is shown by Fig. 38. It has been explained on page 37 that the float rises (or " floats ") as the petrol is turned

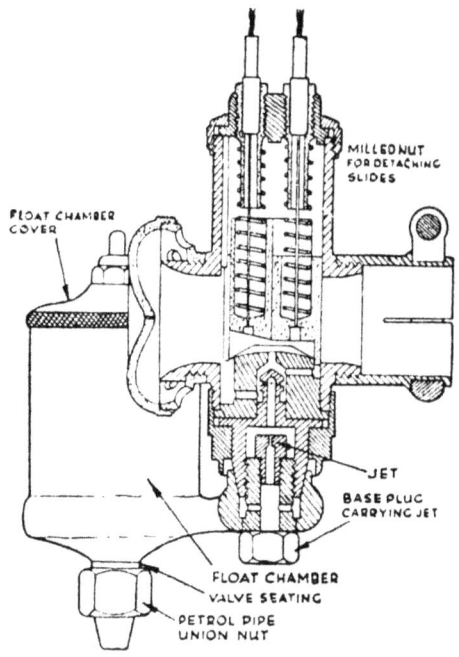

Fig. 38.—Sectional View of the Amac Carburettor

on and shuts off the supply when the proper level in relation to the jet has been fixed. It will also be seen how the air is drawn past the jet and " induces " or sucks the petrol. The air and throttle slides will be noted, as well as how they are controlled.

THE MAGNETO

The magneto, which can be seen in Fig. 37, is driven from the engine shaft, through the timing gear. It consists essentially of a small electric dynamo designed to deliver an electric spark once every two revolutions of the engine. Full particulars regarding adjustments will be found on pages 90 and 91.

Fig. 39.—Details of the Front Fork on the 3·49 h.p. Model

Note the shock absorbers, grease-gun lubrication, and covered brake mechanism

MECHANICAL DETAILS OF THE B.S.A.

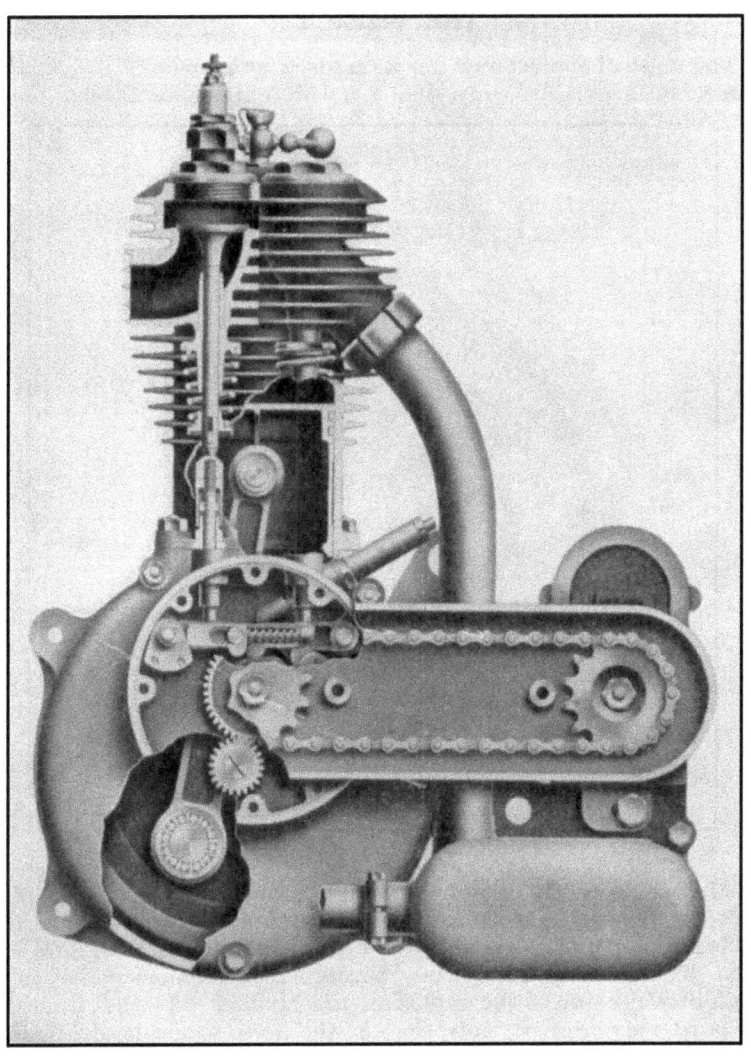

Fig. 40.—Cut-away Detail View of the 5·57 h.p. (1921) Engine, showing Timing Gear

THE SILENCER

The noise of the exhaust gas is reduced by allowing it to expand before it is expelled into the air, this expansion taking place

FIG. 41.—THE QUICKLY-DETACHABLE WHEEL

in the silencer. It is not generally known that the noise of a motor-cycle engine is not caused by the explosion of the gas in the cylinder, but by the exhaust gas being suddenly let loose into the air. The exhaust gas passes through the exhaust valve at a high pressure due to the explosion, and if allowed to pass from the exhaust valve directly into the air, the noise would be deafening. Instead, it passes along the exhaust pipes into the silencer, where it expands and is expelled into the air at a lower pressure.

The silencer has a capacity of four or five times the combustion space.

It is illegal, as pointed out elsewhere, to use a cut-out, that is, a device which enables the exhaust to pass into the air without first passing through the silencer.

MECHANICAL DETAILS OF THE B.S.A.   61

THE FRONT FORKS

Fig. 39, on page 58, shows the type of spring fork fitted to the B.S.A. models. These forks, it is hardly necessary to state, are for purposes of absorbing road shocks, and insulating the rider from the vibration caused. The illustrations are self-explanatory.

FIG. 42.—THE CAMS FOR RAPID CHAIN ADJUSTMENT
The alignment of the wheel is automatic

THE TIMING GEAR

It will have been gathered from the previous chapter that the inlet valve must remain open for about half a revolution of the crank, and the exhaust for a further half revolution. It is the purpose of the timing gear to ensure this, and a cam (see Fig. 40) lifts the inlet valve by means of an adjustable tappet, at the commencement of the suction stroke, and permits it to close at the bottom of the stroke. It does not operate again for $1\frac{1}{2}$ revolutions of the crankshaft. The exhaust valve is similarly operated, commencing to open at about the end of the power stroke.

BRAKES

It is law that two brakes, separately and independently operated, and each capable of stopping the machine, must be fitted. The action and specification, however, has already been given in Chapter I.

THE DETACHABLE WHEEL

A detachable wheel enables the wheel to be removed with the ball-races without interfering with the chain adjustment. The principle adopted is to mount the chain sprocket on ball races on a hollow spindle. Dogs, or other gripping devices, are formed on the sprocket, and identical dogs are formed on the hub, so that the two " marry " or mesh. Similarly, the hub itself is mounted on ball bearings carried on a hollow shaft passing through the hollow shaft of the sprocket, and a long pin is passed through and locked to the fork ends. (See Figs. 41 and 42.)

Shock Absorber. This device has been incorporated with the bottom fork link to enable the deflection and rebound of the fork on rough roads to be controlled. It is adjustable to suit the weight of the rider and the nature of the road surface. To adjust the amount of friction, first slack off the rear nut on left side of fork. Then screw up or undo the bolt to give more or less friction as required, finally locking up the left-hand nut again. The bottom front fork link bolt should be adjusted similarly to the top link bolts.

Grease-Gun Lubrication. A grease-gun is supplied with the kit and this must first be charged with grease. Screw out the T-handle as far as it will go and then unscrew the cap from the barrel at the other end. Fill the barrel with grease and replace the end cap. (This operation is facilitated by the use of Enot's grease-gun filler.) To lubricate, push the nozzle of the gun well down on the nipple, thus opening the valve in the nozzle and the ball valve in the nipple. Now screw down the T-handle a turn or two as required and the grease will be forced into the bearing at high pressure. If the T-handle is stiff, it is a sign that the valve in the gun is still closed, and that it requires forcing further on to the nipple. Owing to the ball valve in nipple, no dust or dirt can enter the bearing and set up a grinding action. When greasing a hub or a point where it is awkward to turn the handle it is suggested that the T-handle be used to press the gun down on to the nipple, while the barrel of the gun is turned to the left to force in the grease.

CHAPTER VI

OVERHAULING

A CAREFUL study of preceding chapters will have given the novice a fair knowledge of the construction of his machine, which, combined with the manipulative skill gained in driving, should enable him to tackle the overhaul of it.

In any case there is the question of simple adjustment, which may become necessary whilst the machine is in use, and the following information has been prepared also to meet that need.

If the engine is running well, it is best for the rider to leave it alone, except for occasionally swilling out the crank-case, as directed under the heading of riding hints.

Testing and Adjusting Tappet Clearance. The clearance between the valve tappets and the valve stems should be checked now and again, though it is unlikely that adjustment will be required unless the valves have been ground in or a new valve fitted. Always test the clearance with the engine warm, and proceed as follows—

First of all make certain that there is clearance between the bottom exhaust tappet nut and the lifting lever. This indicates that the tappet is in proper contact with the cam. It will be obvious that should the flange on the bottom tappet be resting on the lifter lever, it will prevent the tappet from forming proper contact with the cam inside the timing gear, and only partial valve lift will take place, resulting in loss of power, also speed. Turn the engine round by means of the kick-starter, with the decompressor lever down until compression is felt. Then raise the exhaust lifter and push the kick-starter down another couple of inches, so that the piston is at the top of the compression stroke or thereabouts. Now see if there is any clearance between the valve tappets and valve stems. If the clearance is correct, it should be just possible to feel a little motion when the tappet is lifted up and down with the fingers, and it should be possible to pass a piece of the paper on which this book is printed between the head of the tappet and the valve stem, but a stout visiting card should not go through. If the clearance on either valve is not correct, the tappet must be adjusted. To do this, hold the head A by means of the large end of the B.S.A. spanner, and loosen the locking sleeve B (Fig. 43) with the special tappet spanner provided (turning the handle of the spanner to the left). Then screw the head up or down to the required position, and tighten the locking sleeve again by turning the handle of the spanner to the right, meanwhile holding the tappet head A with the B.S.A. spanner, and applying pressure to the left, so as to relieve from strain the small fillets which prevent the tappet rod rotating during adjustment. After tightening up, test the clearance again to make sure that it has not been altered inadvertently while tightening up. It is well worth while taking a little trouble over this tappet adjustment, as on its accuracy depends the silence of the valve gear, as well as the power obtained from the engine.

FIG. 43.—DIAGRAM SHOWING HOW TO ADJUST THE TAPPETS

Decarbonizing the Engine. After 1,500 miles or so have been covered, it may be necessary to decarbonize the engine. The necessity for this will be indicated by the engine becoming very liable to pink or knock, particularly when it is hot. To decarbonize it is first necessary to remove the cylinder. Proceed as follows: Detach the petrol pipe and high tension wire. Take out the sparking plug and valve caps, and remove the compression tap. Remove the exhaust pipe, which is a push fit on the exhaust spigot in 2·49, 3·49 and 4·93 h.p. models, supported by a clip on the crank-case, and a push fit in the silencer. (In other models a screw connection is used.) Remove the carburettor by unscrewing the clip bolt on the connection between the carburettor and the cylinder. This bolt can be unscrewed by means of the small end of the B.S.A. spanner, and when it is loose the carburettor can be slid off backwards. It is as well to tie the carburettor up out of the way, preferably to the carrier stays. Now remove the four nuts which hold the cylinder to the crank case. Lift the cylinder up and backwards into the rear angle of the frame, and then turn the engine forwards until the piston comes out of the bottom of the cylinder, steadying the piston as it emerges, so that it shall not fall over and get cracked when it comes clear of the cylinder. Assistance will be needed for this operation.

Removing the Carbon. Remove the valves from the cylinder and carefully chip out all carbon from the top of the cylinder and the valve pocket and passages with a long-handled screwdriver. After all the carbon has been removed, swill out with paraffin and then wipe the cylinder thoroughly with a clean but oily rag immediately before reassembling. After scraping carbon off the piston, finish by polishing the top of the piston lightly with fine emery paper or metal polish, taking care not to scratch the side of the cylinder.

Examining and Removing Piston Rings. Now examine the piston rings. If they are bright and quite free in their grooves, it is better to leave them alone, as they are very brittle, and there is a considerable risk of breaking them during removal. If there are any brown patches on the rings remove them in the manner shown by F.g. 44, and fit new ones. If the rings are stuck in their grooves, prise them out very carefully and clean them,

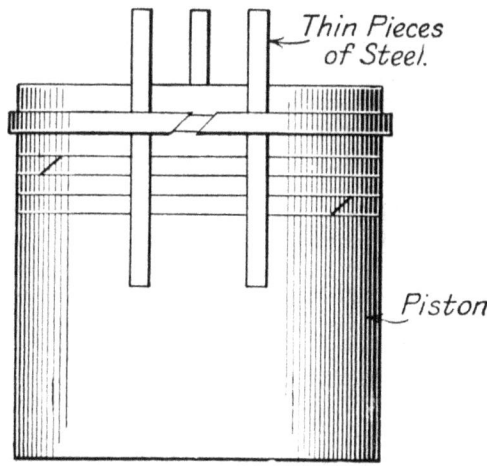

FIG. 44.—HOW TO REMOVE PISTON RINGS

after soaking in paraffin to soften the carbon. Scrape any carbon from the grooves and from the inside and edges of the rings, and then replace, providing they are otherwise in order. If, however, the machine is used for speed work, the lower piston ring may be discarded with advantage.

Position of Piston Ring Gaps. After cleaning the piston, make sure that the slots in the piston rings are on the opposite sides of the piston to one another, and then smear the sides of the piston generously with engine oil, to obviate any risk of damage when first running after assembly.

Cleaning Out the Crankcase. While the cylinder is off, it is advisable to clean out the crankcase. This is done by unscrewing the drain plug on the bottom right-hand side of the crankcase and allowing the oil to drain out. The crankcase should then be swilled out with paraffin and the plug replaced. Make sure that the latter is screwed up tight.

Reassembling the Engine. After all this has been done, the engine may be reassembled. Hold the cylinder in the rear angle of the frame and place the piston a little before bottom dead centre on the downward stroke. The cylinder should then slide home quite easily. Replace the cylinder nuts, making sure they are tight, and then fit the valve caps and compression tap. The carburettor petrol pipe, high tension wire, and exhaust pipe may then be replaced.

Running the Engine After Assembly. Before starting up the engine open the valve fully on the oil sight drip feed on the oil tank, and give at least three complete charges of lubricating oil to the engine. This is very important and must be kept in mind. After this has been done, adjust the oil valve to give its usual supply of oil, according to whether the machine is used for sidecar or solo work respectively.

The engine should then be ready for the road again, but full power cannot be expected until it has had a little running in to allow valves and piston rings to become properly bedded in.

Valve Timing. The valve timing of the engine should not be tampered with in any way, as the makers' setting is that which has been found to give the best results. Should the timing be disturbed, however, the engine should be revolved until the tooth on the small pinion, with a dash mark on it, is at the top. The inlet cam pinion should then be inserted in such a way that the space, also marked with a dash, is occupied by the marked tooth on the small pinion. The space on exhaust cam pinion marked with a dot should then be engaged with the tooth also marked with a dot on the inlet pinion.

How to Grind-in the Valves. If either of the valves is slightly pitted on its seat it may be ground in by smearing the coned faces with a coarse emery paste, replacing the valve on its seat, and rotating the valve on it by means of a screwdriver placed in the slot in the crown of the valve. This will rapidly effect the removal of uneven places, and when an even surface shows the faces should be wiped clean and a thin even paste of flour emery applied. Rotate the valve as before by means of the screwdriver until a dead smooth surface results. If it is badly pitted, however, it should be sent to the B.S.A. works at Redditch to be refaced. On its return a very slight amount of grinding in will be sufficient

OVERHAULING

to make a good face. Never attempt to grind in a badly pitted valve, as excessive valve grinding wears away the valve seat in the cylinder and causes the valve to become pocketed with consequent loss of power. (See Fig. 45.) After grinding in, be very careful to wipe away all traces of the grinding material, both on the valve and in the cylinder.

Magneto Timing. To re-time the magneto, first loosen the chain sprocket, remove the contact breaker cover and compression tap. Rotate the engine in a forward direction until the inlet valve closes. Now insert a rod or wire through the compression tap hole, and move the engine still further, until the piston is felt to be at the top of its stroke. Move the contact breaker by means of the control lever until the platinum points are just about

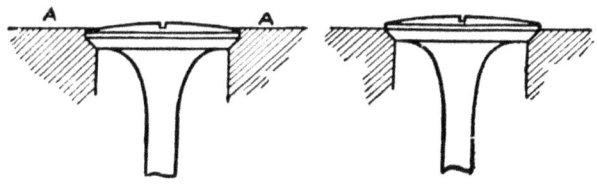

FIG. 45.—DIAGRAM SHOWING HOW VALVES BECOME POCKETED AFTER FREQUENT REGRINDING

to break. Lightly tighten the magneto sprocket and then check the timing by again finding the top of the compression stroke and examining the position of points. If correct, finally tighten up sprocket nut.

Adjusting the Magneto Chain. To adjust magneto chain, slacken the two bolts at side of magneto platform and remove chain cover plate. Now slide magneto backward or forward to required position and tighten up bolts. Afterwards test the chain tension. This should be such that the slightest possible amount of up and down movement can be felt in centre of chain. If the chain is too tight, a grinding noise will be noticeable, while too slack a chain will cause a rattling noise.

Adjusting the Magneto. This requires no lubrication whatever. Test the clearance between the contact points P (Fig. 46) by means of the gauge attached to magneto spanner. If incorrect, adjust the point, first releasing the lock nut at end of pin opposite to contact. Occasionally clean the points by brushing over with petrol applied with a small brush.

Sparking Plug. Clean the sparking plug points occasionally and adjust the gap to between $\frac{1}{64}$ in. and $\frac{1}{32}$ in. Make the gap as large as possible, however, consistent with easy starting, as a wide spark gap means a hot spark, which, in turn, ensures satisfactory running, and lessens the tendency for the points to become sooted up.

Care of Chains. It is advisable to remove both chains periodically. Remove chains by detaching the spring link. They should then be thoroughly cleansed in petrol or paraffin and dried off.

Fig. 46.—The Make-and-Break Portion of the Magneto; P = Contact Points

Immerse them for some time at about the temperature of boiling water in a mixture of grease and graphite. After they have cooled wipe off the excess lubricant. Under load the lubricant will be gradually squeezed out; the process should therefore be repeated, say, every 1,000 miles. Clean the sprockets, and on replacing the chain note that the split end of the spring fastener is at the rear to direction of travel of chain.

Adjusting the Front Driving Chain. To adjust the front driving chain, loosen the two nuts L on clamping bolts (Fig. 47) and slide the gear box backwards or forwards as required. The chain, when properly adjusted, should have about $\frac{1}{4}$ in. sag or drop at centre. If a considerable movement has been made in the position of gear box, it will be necessary to re-adjust the gear control rod. To effect this, the lever should be moved towards front of machine until the spring plunger inside gear box can be felt to have registered with its recess (lever will now be approximately in the upright position). The nuts C should now be slackened from sleeve D, bearing in mind that the lower one has

OVERHAULING

a left-hand thread. Sleeve *D* should now be moved until operating lever *A* is just making contact with the end of its quadrant, as at *E*. Then tighten nuts *C*. Test adjustment by moving lever to middle of neutral position, noting that the spring plunger

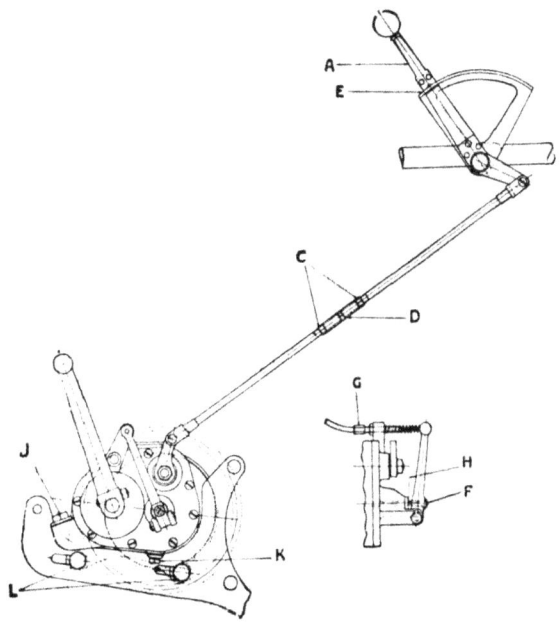

Fig. 47.—How to Adjust the Front Chain

can be felt engaging when the lever *A* is opposite the respective position on the quadrant. The clutch can be adjusted by means of either screw *F* or *G*, the lock-nuts having first been released. The screws should then be adjusted until a slight clearance is perceptible between screw *F* and rod *H*.

Adjusting the Rear Chain. To adjust the rear chain (or in the case of the chain-cum-belt model, the belt), loosen the nut on the hub spindle on the left side of the machine; then the nut on the right side. Apply an adjustable spanner (handle upwards) to the square end of the hub spindle, then turn towards the front of the machine until the chain is tight. Slightly turn the reverse way to slacken the chain sufficiently to ensure free running. Hold the spanner firmly in this position, keeping the cams (see Fig. 42) and blocks in close contact, then with the other spanner tighten the left-hand nut, remove the adjustable spanner and tighten up the right-hand spindle nut. This chain should have a sag of about ½ in. when properly adjusted.

Adjusting the Brake. It may be found necessary to adjust the rear brake after adjusting this chain. To accomplish this, remove the screw in the toggle end of brake-rod which holds the brake-shoe lever to rod. Loosen the lever fulcrum nut in the slotted lug on the chain stay, and slide the brake-shoe forward or backward as required until the brake-pad touches the side of the brake rim. Then withdraw it just sufficiently to allow of the wheel being revolved freely without the pad touching the brake-drum at any point; now lock it in position. Unscrew the two lock-nuts at either side of the adjusting sleeve on rod, bearing in mind that the nut on the shorter rod is screwed left-hand, and turn the latter right or left-hand as required, to permit of the rod and brake-shoe being again coupled up. Finally, screw up the lock-nuts on either side of the adjusting sleeve.

Adjusting the Clutch. When the chain case is removed, the spring pressure of clutch may be adjusted if the cap on the clutch cover plate is taken off, which is done by removing the nuts provided for the purpose. This will disclose the adjusting nut. If it is required to increase the spring pressure turn in a clockwise direction with the spanner provided. To make clutch sweeter in action, a half turn or so in the opposite direction will be required. To dismantle clutch, the nut must be removed. The end plate and spring will now slide off, leaving the plates accessible. Thoroughly cleanse by means of a stiff brush and petrol, removing all trace of oil or grease, and when dry re-assemble. Refit the cap and make sure that the nuts are tight. Details of the mechanical arrangement of the clutch will be found on pages 49 and 53 and details of operation on page 21.

Cleaning the Machine. The life of the machine is increased and its appearance and value greatly improved by regular and careful attention to cleaning. Especial care should be taken near all moving parts, so as to prevent grit working in and causing undue wear and other troubles. Particularly is this the case round the front, rear, and sidecar hubs, carburettor, magneto, valve stems, tappets, front brake and gear box. Never remove dry and caked mud from the frame, mudguards, etc. To do so means that the enamel will be subjected to the abrasive action of the grit, and the polish will soon be destroyed. Thoroughly soak the dirt first, then wash it off and wipe the parts dry. If a hosepipe is available, this will be found the most satisfactory

OVERHAULING

way of removing dirt. Direct the stream of water on the portion being cleaned, taking care to avoid playing direct on to the hub bearings, etc. Afterwards brush lightly with a soft brush, finally drying and polishing with chamois leather. To remove dirt from the engine, soak it well with paraffin and cleanse with a fresh supply, then wipe dry. To remove oil stains from the crankcase use caustic soda solution. An occasional coating of a cylinder paint should be given to prevent rusting of the cylinder, or a solution of lamp black in paraffin to which a small quantity of gold size has been added may be used. This will also be found to assist the radiation of heat.

The Front Forks. Lubricate the front fork link bearings frequently.

Keep the link bolts tight enough to eliminate side-play, which generally causes a mechanical click. To adjust, unscrew the nuts on the left-hand side and screw up the bolts from the right-hand side just sufficiently tight to eliminate all side play, then lock in position with the nuts, doing one bolt at a time. If too tight the flexibility of the fork will be reduced.

To Remove the Front Fork Spring. Support the crankcase on a box, so that the front wheel stands clear of the ground. Remove the nut from top spring retaining bolt, and depress same until it can be removed from anchorage lug, afterwards "unwinding" spring from bottom retaining scroll. Then remove the four bolts from the forks by unscrewing the nuts on the left-hand side and withdrawing from the right. Slide out the four links sideways and the forks will fall clear of the machine and the spring may be lifted off.

The Steering Head. Frequent attention should also be paid to the steering head. A lubricator is fitted on the right-hand side at the bottom of ball head, and thin oil should preferably be used. If this point is not oiled regularly the head will become stiff and the steering will feel unsteady. Therefore oil regularly. To adjust head, unscrew the clip nut, screw down the adjusting nut by means of a special spanner supplied with tool kit, until there is no perceptible shake in head, slack back about a twelfth of a turn, and then screw up clip nut again tightly.

Lubricating the Gear. The efficiency and life of the gear will be greatly increased if the following instructions are carefully adhered to. Remove the oil plugs, already referred to, on end plate of gear box to drain the old oil out, and inject B.S.A. special cylinder or gear box oil until the oil level rises to the top of filler hole when machine is in upright position. This level should be maintained by frequent injections. After every 1,500 miles running, thoroughly flush with paraffin. To do this the machine should be started on stand, high gear afterwards being engaged with clutch in. Remove the gear box cover and pour in clean paraffin. With the engine running the gears will be swilled clean, and the paraffin should be drained out by means of the drain plug. Carefully drain by means of the plug provided, afterwards refilling with oil to the correct level. Care should be taken that the clearance between screw F and rod H is maintained (see instructions for adjusting) otherwise the full spring pressure will not be operating on the plates, and clutch will be continually slipping.

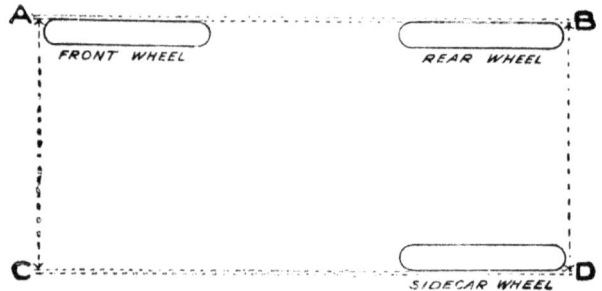

FIG. 48.—HOW TO ALIGN THE SIDECAR

Pipe Joints. It is essential that the whole of the joints of the pipes, etc., made between the tank, sight feed, and engine, should be quite airtight, and in the event of a collection of oil in the sight feed which fails to clear itself, the non-return washer, situated under the sight feed, should be inspected. This non-return washer consists of a small pen-steel disc working in a brass socket and prevents blow back from the engine. It will be necessary in this case to ascertain that this has not become displaced or has been prevented from properly seating itself through dirty or congealed oil. The parts in question should be cleaned and the final delivery pipe should also be inspected for a partial stoppage when this trouble will, without doubt, be overcome.

Alignment of the B.S.A. Sidecar. The 4·93 h.p. and higher powered models only are designed for a sidecar, connections being formed integral with the frame.

It is essential for the life of the machine that the sidecar is correctly aligned and Fig. 48 shows how this should be carried out. Lay a long wooden straight edge ($A-B$) along both wheels

OVERHAULING

of the motor-bicycle, and a similar straight edge (*C–D*) along the sidecar wheel. Make certain that the machine is perfectly upright; then adjust the sidecar until the points *A* and *C* are exactly the same distance apart as the points *B* and *D*, that is, the straight edges should be parallel.

For the purpose of alignment, the main sidecar connection is provided with adjusting washers, two of which are at the chassis end of the main front arm and four on the footboard

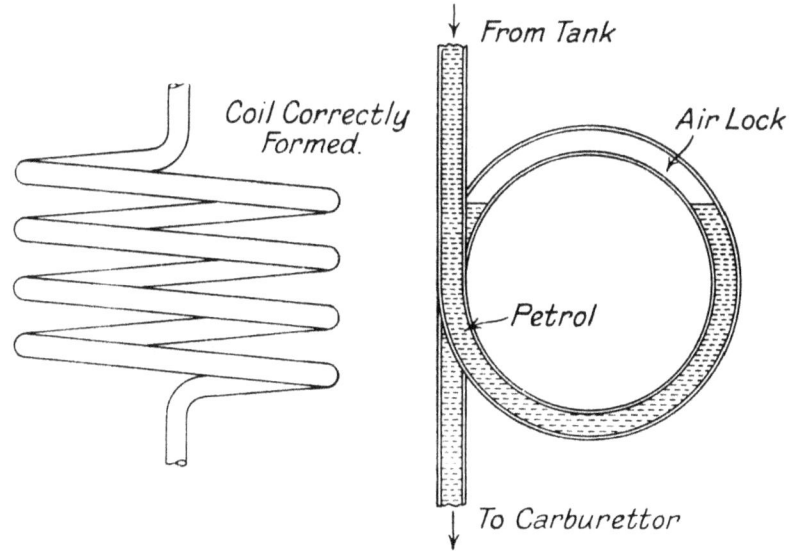

FIGS. 49 AND 50.—THE CORRECT AND INCORRECT METHODS OF COILING PETROL PIPES

connection. These are supplied loose and are to be used in lining up the machine, if necessary, to obtain the correct alignment as the diagram above.

The rear connection is fitted with spherical washer and spring washer to facilitate the vertical alignment of the machine. Lock up tightly after the correct alignment has been obtained. It is important that any vertical alignment should be released at the bolts on the twin tubes of the chassis.

Care should be taken to refit all castellated nuts with split cotter pins.

Coiling Petrol Pipes. Figs. 49 and 50 show the correct and incorrect methods of forming the coils in petrol pipes. It will be noticed that air lock (a common trouble) is caused when the coils are formed with a horizontal axis. They should, of course, have a vertical axis.

Removing Tight Studs. Fig. 51 shows the method of removing studs for purposes of replacement. Two nuts are locked together, and a spanner used on the *bottom* one to unscrew the stud.

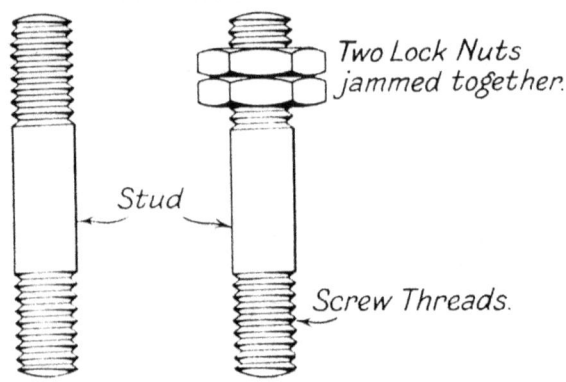

FIG. 51.—HOW TO REMOVE STUDS

Paper Washers. These are useful in preventing leakage, and may be made by placing a sheet of paper over the part for which the washer is intended and rubbing round the edge. A clear impression is thus made on the paper.

Truing Wheels. The preliminary operation is first to ascertain the extent of warp or deviation from the circular, and this is done by spinning the rim between the forks, holding a piece of chalk to the rim, so that the hit-and-miss places are clearly marked. Where the rim rises and falls, the spokes at those parts must be respectively tightened or slackened. If the wheel is " out of flat " (lack of truth sideways) the spokes must be tightened on one side and loosened on the other. It is a fiddling operation requiring great care. A nipple key should be used for turning the nipples.

Having trued the wheels sideways and circumferentially, pass a cord through the spokes and stretch it taut so that it lies diagonally across the oil-hole of the hub, so that it touches the rim on opposing sides. Next reverse the position of the diagonal, so that it touches the other two opposing sides. If the wheel is not pulled over on the hub, the string should pass through the centre of the oil-hole in both instances.

The spokes when plucked with the fingers should all yield the same note. If at any time it is necessary to remove the rim from the spokes, perhaps to change rims or remove a dent, and the rider is uncertain about wheel building, before removing the nipples obtain some fine copper wire and tie the spokes together at the point where they intercept one another. Then remove the nipples and carefully spring the spokes out of place, which will leave them in their proper position on the hub.

Re-enamelling. With so many excellent enamels on the market, the amateur can obtain excellent results if at the time of overhauling he considers the frame needs enamelling. If time and expense warrants it, he is, however, advised to have it stoved, a special process of *baking* the enamel on which cannot be done at home without special plant. The frame should be stripped of fittings and scraped down to the bare metal with an old knife, or the edge of a piece of glass, and then polished absolutely bright and smooth with emery cloth. This is important, for any imperfections in the surface, such as roughness or rust, will affect the finished surface.

Then give a coat of enamel of the desired colour. When this is thoroughly dry, dull its surface with very fine glasspaper, and apply a second coat. Repeat this process until four or five coats have been applied, when a coat of varnish should be evenly brushed on and left to get thoroughly hard.

The work should be carried out in a warm room or shed, and when applying the varnish, the floor should be sprinkled with water to lay the dust.

The varnish should be left to dry, keeping doors and windows shut to exclude all dust, which, if allowed to enter, will settle on the varnish, causing the latter to dry with a gritty surface.

Lining transfers are on the market, and if used should be applied before the coat of varnish.

CHAPTER VII

RUNNING COSTS

THE aim of this chapter is to show the costs when the machine is run economically.

Costs to be Met. The actual cost of the machine, the accessories, registration and driving licences may be considered as a first cost. Apart from this, the depreciation, running repairs, and running costs must be met. Petrol, oil, spares, garage and plugs are the main items.

Petrol Consumption. On a single-cylinder engine of from 2 h.p. to 3 h.p. (solo) the machine should run at least 80 miles to the gallon, and when specially tuned, should do from 90 to 110 miles. The mileage per gallon is not in direct proportion to the power; if a machine of 3 h.p. does 90 miles to the gallon, a 6 h.p. will do more than 45.

A 4 h.p. machine should do at least 60 m.p.g., and an 8 h.p. at least 40, it being presumed that a sidecar is fitted to them. Ridden solo, of course, a greater m.p.g. would be obtained.

It must be pointed out, however, that factors may enter the question, and cause a variation in petrol consumption. For example, constant driving on low gear will cause excessive consumption of petrol, and so will too large a jet, hilly country, bad roads, the weather, etc.

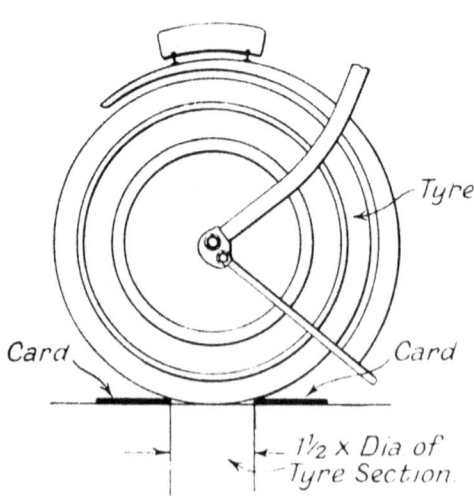

FIG. 52.—AN EXCELLENT METHOD OF CHECKING TYRE PRESSURES BY MEANS OF TWO CARDS

Oil Consumption. One quart of oil should be sufficient for at least 500 miles (bearing in mind the last sentence of the preceding paragraph) of a solo machine up to 3 h.p., and at least 350 on the higher powers mentioned.

Tyres. The makers usually supply tyres of sufficient size for the purpose of the machine, and if kept inflated to the proper pressure should have an effective life of from 4,000 to 8,000 miles. The pressure may be tested, as shown in Fig. 52, by means of two cards. The machine should be loaded before taking the measurements, and if it is ascertained when the tyre is inflated to the proper and known pressure, the data can be used for future reference.

To run tyres under-inflated is considerably to lessen their life, and over-inflated is to sacrifice comfort. Obviously luck enters the question, for a brand new tyre may be badly cut on the first ride. Vulcanizing is so far advanced, however, and the re-treading of tyres such a successful process, that tyre costs of recent years have been much reduced. A worn and weak back tyre should not be discarded, for it will serve satisfactorily on the sidecar wheel or front wheel long after it has ceased to be safe enough to take the greater load of the back wheel. The transmission of motor cycles being by means of the back wheel, that tyre obviously will wear out; and requires to be heavier than the other two.

In order to prolong the life of the tyres, it is advisable to go over the tread occasionally and pick out with a wire pricker any pieces of flint which may have become embedded. The holes should be filled with the special stopping sold for the purpose—it costs but a few pence.

Sparking Plugs. Always use plugs of the detachable-centre type, as new centres may be obtained, which is a cheaper procedure than buying a new plug. A reputable make, though dearer to buy, is cheaper in the long run, for they last sometimes for years with an occasional clean. Certainly not more than one new plug a year should be necessary. The reach of the plug (see Fig. 53) is of importance—one with too long a reach may cause serious damage.

Garage. A solo machine should not cost more than 2s. 6d. per week and a combination more than 3s. 6d. per week. If the machine is accommodated for only an evening or so, the rate may be 1s. per night or thereabouts. It is important to remember that agents for the clubs mentioned earlier have a schedule of charges which is conspicuously posted up in their garages, and it is useful to inspect this and politely offer the scheduled amount. If your costs are to be kept low, deal only with reputable agents —not back-street firms.

These charges, be it known, are also fixed for cleaning the machine, and other items.

If one has facilities, of course, the machine may be stored at home (especially if a solo mount), when this item of cost vanishes. Or if one has available garden space, the many cheap portable sheds, specially marketed for the purpose, are worth considering.

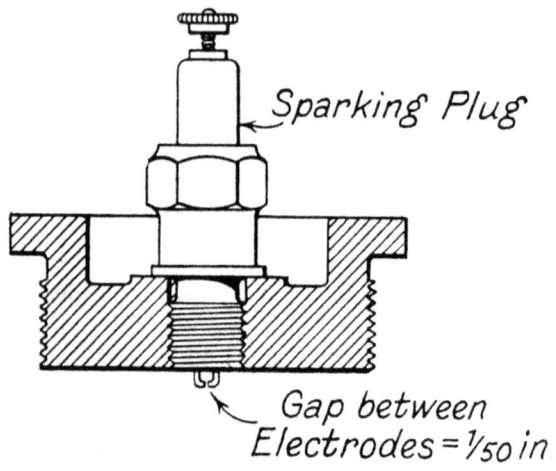

Fig. 53.—Diagram Illustrating Reach of Sparking Plug

Maintenance of Lamps. Carbide is largely used for headlamps; this should be purchased in 14 lb. lots, a much cheaper method than buying it 1 lb. at a time. The cost of the head and tail lamp, if worked from one generator, is practically negligible, for only for a part of the year is it necessary to use lamps. If the Magdyno outfit, as supplied by the B.S.A. and fitted if desired as an extra, the cost of lamps is negligible, for the current for all lamps is generated from a small dynamo driven from the engine. With a sidecar machine it is usual to run the sidecar lamp and rear lamp from an accumulator carried in the sidecar locker. Two accumulators should be purchased, so that one may be kept on charge whilst the other is in use. Accumulators should always be kept on charge, or they rapidly deteriorate and become useless. When not in use, alternate slow charging and discharging keeps them in good condition. Dry cells are not recommended. Three

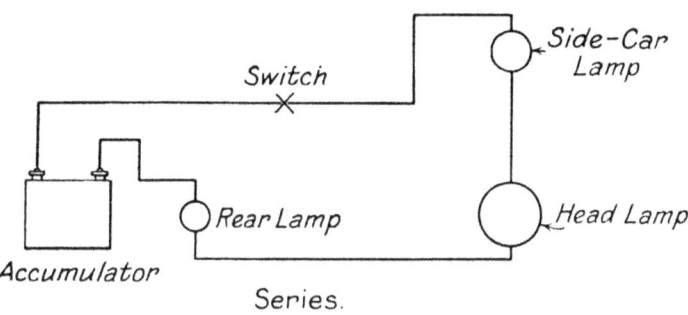
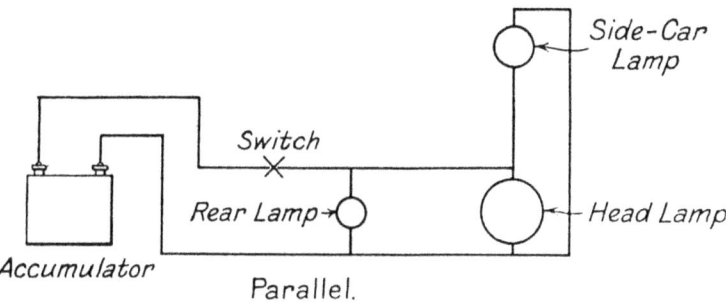
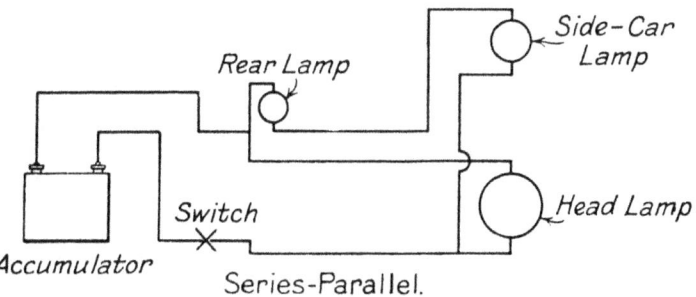

Fig. 54.—Wiring Diagrams for Electric Lights

systems of wiring are given in Fig. 54. The cost of accumulator charging for the year is quite small—certainly not more than 15s.

Depreciation. This ugly item is an added reason for buying a reputable machine in the first place, for such is always readily saleable at a fair second-hand price. For the first year a depreciation of 20 per cent of the purchase price should be allowed, in two years 30 per cent, in three years 35 per cent, in four years 40 per cent, and any period over that from 50 per cent. In reckoning the cost of motor-cycling, this factor must be taken into consideration. Reckless or careless driving is likely to make motor-cycling a costly affair, as well as unpopular, and the hint should be sufficient.

CHAPTER VIII

TOURING

MOTOR-cycle touring to-day is almost as certain as travelling by railway, and is, if anything, less costly and certainly much healthier. There is the added pleasure of being able to vary one's rate of progress at will—lingering amongst pleasant scenery and hurrying through the drab portions. The important questions are those of dress, luggage, tools, equipment, maps and guides.

DRESS

Personal comfort is of first importance, and all the delights of the weather and the countryside are liable to be lost sight of if it is not attained. It is wise to remember the humour and even contempt with which a certain type of motor-cyclist is regarded. You know the sort—the owner of one of the lightest of light-weights who will dash round the country at the alarming rate of about 12 miles an hour, clad in a heavy leather suit, goggles, heavy crash helmet and wellingtons. Do not follow his example. Select your dress with due regard to utility, comfort and appearance. There is little need to provide special clothing for pottering. Protection from dust is all that is needed, and a light coat of the dustproof variety fills the bill. Apart from penetrating one's clothing, dust can also produce painful results if a sharp piece gets under the eyelids, and for this reason goggles are an essential part of the equipment. One's ordinary clothes may be used, but there is always the risk of splashing them with oil, or otherwise spoiling them. It is cheaper in the long run, if a great deal of riding is to be done, to have a special dress consisting of riding breeches and leggings or stockings, the dustproof coat (of the sports coat type) and goggles.

Goggles. A word or so here about goggles is advisable. Goggles are obtainable in a variety of forms, from the one-piece celluloid pattern to the spectacle type having two oval lenses, which may be replaced when broken. The former, the writer finds, are extremely comfortable to wear, and as well the field of vision is not so restricted as with the lens type. Goggles with tinted glasses are also available, and in bright sunlight are extremely restful to the eyes. One has only to ride with the sun glaring in one's eyes for any distance to realize what " sun-blindness " is, and the feeling of helplessness which accompanies it. These coloured glasses (blue and yellow are useful colours) lessen the possibility of this.

Another type of goggles which has the laudable object of saving the eyes of the rider in the event of accident is the Triplex goggles. Each lens of this consists of two layers of glass with a layer of celluloid between, and although in the case of an accident they may crack, they do not actually break.

There is another point connected with goggles which receives all too little attention. It is the *fit* of them. Goggles which do not fit closely to the face will cause colds in the eyes and eye soreness, and even dust may enter the eye. See to it, then, that the goggles fit close to the face.

All Weather Riding. Whilst it cannot be gainsaid that spring and summer riding is pleasanter, autumn and winter riding, providing the day is not wet, is not without its charm.

Warmth is the main consideration, and we shall now show how to attain this.

Winter clothing is certainly on a more elaborate scale than summer clothing. Underclothing, which in summer is of the light " summer-weight " variety, should be of the heavy woollen winter quality. The commonest type of winter dress, and one which withal is the cheapest, consists of the ordinary buff waterproof coat and leggings, the latter lacing or buttoning up the sides. They may be purchased from most accessory dealers. An objection to them is that they soon show grease marks, and even when fitting nicely lack that smart appearance which the average motor cyclist requires. Another objection is the awkward operation of lacing or buttoning the leggings, especially if the fingers are cold.

A much more satisfactory " all weather " apparel consists of a brown oilskin coat, of such a length that it barely covers the knees. To have it longer is to make kick-starting awkward, and to run the risk of portions getting caught in the transmission or spokes. Two patterns are made—one which buttons together and one which straps together. The writer prefers the latter, as it is possible to pull it more closely to the body, under which condition it is warmer and excludes penetrating draughts.

The apparel for the legs to be worn with the oilskin for winter riding may consist of that already recommended, but undoubtedly the best form of mud and water excluder is a pair of waders, which somewhat resemble fishermen's waders. They may appear ungainly, but they do keep one dry, and enable one to arrive at the destination clean and dry underneath, and there is no risk of the trousers becoming soiled.

Overall suits of light material enable one's ordinary attire to be worn underneath, and upon arriving at the home of, say, one's sweetheart, it is merely necessary to remove the overalls to present a spick and span appearance. If anything, they are more suited to summer riding, but plenty of riders wear them all the year round.

Headwear. It has already been stated that a cap is most satisfactory, and it should be of such a fit that it may be worn peak to the front, with little risk of being blown off. Some riders wear caps peak to the back, for one of two reasons. Either the cap is too large and blows off when correctly worn, or they wish in their vanity to be regarded as racing motor cyclists. The peak helps to keep the sun from the eyes, and its only objection is that it is in the way when raising the goggles.

A felt hat of the soft, or trilby, pattern is comfortable if of good fit, and is cooler to wear in summer than a cap.

The helmet undoubtedly is advisable for those who intend to ride long distances in all weathers, for while it must be admitted that some wear them to " look the part," it is entirely wrong to assume that only racing men should wear them. They are preferred because they are extremely comfortable in use, eliminate the whistle of the wind past one's ears when travelling in a wind or at fairly high speed, are quite weatherproof, and do not blow off. Helmets of the crash type are intended for competition work, and for such are advised. Those likely to have much riding to do in wet weather may find the fisherman's " sou'-wester," perhaps, even more serviceable than a helmet.

Several other garments are marketed. Woollen cardigans having long sleeves, and intended to be worn in conjunction with sleeved leather waistcoats are intended as aids to warmth. In all cases avoid the loud extreme, if you do not wish to be a standing joke among your friends.

Gloves. The problem of keeping the hands warm and at the same time enabling them to finger the controls sensitively, is a difficult one. Ordinary fleece-lined gloves allow the air to blow up the sleeve. To obviate this, gauntlets may be worn. These have an extension which fits over the coat sleeve. The difficulty with gloves and gauntlets, however, is that the fingers " fumble " the controls, and are not nearly so sensitive.

The writer does not recommend woollen gloves, for they are liable to become caught in the controls and, say, drag the throttle lever open at the very moment when it is desired to be closed.

An attempt to solve the glove difficulty has been made by one or two firms who market a rubber muff, like the extension of the gauntlet glove. This fits over and beyond the grips of the handlebars, so that the hands are sheltered and the wind deflected.

Leg Shields. The obvious object of these is to keep the clothing clean and dry and in muddy weather they undoubtedly do keep a considerable amount off, but the very wide and efficient mudguarding of the B.S.A. machine renders their use almost unnecessary. They usually screw on to the footboards and clip on to the frame.

Windscreens. Lately windscreens have been marketed which attach to the handlebars and prevent the face from getting cold.

LUGGAGE

The question of what luggage to carry on a tour depends to a great extent on the length of the tour and the type of machine. The point of view to adopt is : What can I do without ? Not what can I do with.

For a week-end tour one obviously must take night attire, a clean shirt and vest, two clean collars (to provide a margin for accidents with greasy fingers), shaving tackle, tooth brush, brush and comb, soft hat or cap, and socks. With regard to clothing, although space may be found for it, it is well to travel in the suit one desires to wear, and to protect it in the manner already noted under " Dress." It must be remembered that on a solo machine only a small suit case can be accommodated, as only the carrier is available for it, but with a sidecar, even though a passenger be carried, there is the additional space afforded by the locker, and small items can easily be accommodated in with the passenger. All bags should be packed as tightly as possible to avoid damage by road vibration.

If the tour is to last for a week or a fortnight, carry only sufficient clothing for immediate needs, and arrange for underclothing, etc., to be sent on to an appropriate destination, returning the soiled apparel by the same means.

INCIDENTAL MATTERS

Spares. There is little need to carry more than a repair outfit, pump, usual tools, as supplied with the machine, spare plugs, spare tubes, spare chains (or chain and belt) and chain extractor or belt punch, and spare valves and valve springs.

TOURING

Useful oddments such as cones, bolts, nuts, chain-coupling links, insulating tape, electric bulbs and/or burners can be packed in a small box with pieces of rag stuffed between to prevent rattle and damage.

Maps and Guides. These are quite a necessary adjunct to touring, and indeed the fascination of planning a tour is part of its pleasure. The route should be traced out in red ink on the map, and the sidecar passenger is then able to direct the driver by following the map in conjunction with the direction taken. A contour road book is useful, in that it enables one to pick the flattest route. Ordnance survey maps are recommended, or Bartholomew's, and a scale of one mile or two miles to the inch is preferred. So complete and comprehensive are these maps that finding one's way is simplicity itself. It should here be mentioned that Messrs. Michelin publish an excellent road guide almost indispensable to the tourist, for in it is a list of the hotels and repairers for every village and town in the United Kingdom. Additionally, the distance from one town to another is given, and street plans of important towns are presented. It is a wonderful compilation, deservedly popular and quite interesting to read. The Dunlop Tyre Company issue a work of equal merit, and either of the volumes can be recommended.

The Tour in Prospect. If the reader is considering a tour and is a member of one of the Associations mentioned in Chapter II, it is well to remember that these offer special touring facilities to their members, and accordingly the secretary should be apprised of the intended route. Especially is this necessary when a Continental tour is to be undertaken, for the Society sees to the obtaining of the members' passports, carnets or triptiques, and renders unnecessary the leaving of deposits when going into a foreign land to satisfy legal requirements regarding the law of imports and exports.

Taking the Machine Abroad. The triptique referred to in the last paragraph enables the owner to travel in Finland, Holland, France, Italy, Switzerland, Belgium, Portugal, Spain, Rumania, Russia, Norway and Sweden, or as an alternative they can be equipped with an International Customs Pass, issued by the A.C.U. and A.A. to members and non-members, whereby the highest continental duty payable suffices for all the countries forming part of the convention.

International Travelling Passes (lasting 12 months) are also issued, enabling the holders to travel in all countries which are parties to the agreement, without obtaining special licences or carrying special numbers in each country as hitherto. The Customs Pass concerns the customs duty payable ; the Travelling Pass is exclusively a licence for the machine and driver abroad.

Up-to-date information about the best means of transit and the best routes is also supplied, and may save a lot of trouble.

It is not nowadays required of the tourist to submit to being examined by a foreign official, to obtain foreign licences, temporary foreign number or any other of the onerous formalities. It is only necessary to obtain the International pass, and fix an oval plate to the machine with the letters G.B. painted in white on a black ground. This plate must be illuminated at night.

Continental Rule of the Road, etc. As a general rule *Keep to the Left* and *Pass on the Right* in Austria-Hungary, Portugal and Sweden.

As a general rule *Keep to the Right* and *Pass on the Left* in Belgium, France, Germany, Holland, Italy, Russia, Spain, Switzerland, and the following provinces of Austria-Hungary, viz., Carniola, Carinthia, Dalmatia, Istria and Tyrol.

The speed limit in Belgium is 40 kilom. an hour in the country, and 15 in town. Special regulations apply to Brussels. Motorcycles may use the paths made specially for cyclists. The Belgian roads (except in some districts) are exceedingly bad.

Lamps must be lit in France not later than fifteen minutes after sunset. A *green* light, in the case of motor-cars, should be shown in front on the left, and it is compulsory to carry an efficient tail light on the left-hand side to illuminate clearly the back number plates at night time.

Normally the majority of French roads are very good. Cars and motor-cycles entering Paris are stopped, the petrol in the tanks is measured, and *octroi* duty charged.

The roads in Holland are generally good, but narrow and winding. No speed limit is fixed on country roads, but motorists can be charged with driving to the common danger. Some roads are closed to motor traffic.

The general rule of the road in Italy is to keep to the right, but it is frequently reversed in many districts and in many towns.

In Northern Italy and parts of Central Italy, the roads are good and sometimes excellent : in the Southern Provinces the roads are bad.

The speed limit in Spain is 12 kilom. ($7\frac{1}{4}$ miles) per hour.

LIGHTING-UP TIME TABLE, 1926

(Greenwich Mean Time)

Add One Hour during Summer Time Period

January

1	4.30 p.m.	18	4.52 p.m.
4	4.33 ,,	22	4.59 ,,
8	4.38 ,,	25	5. 4 ,,
12	4.42 ,,	29	5.11 ,,
15	4.48 ,,		

February

2	5.17 p.m.	15	5.44 p.m.
5	5.26 ,,	19	5.52 ,,
8	5.31 ,,	22	5.57 ,,
12	5.39 ,,	26	6. 3 ,,

March

1	6. 8 p.m.	18	6.37 p.m.
4	6.13 ,,	22	6.44 ,,
8	6.20 ,,	25	6.49 ,,
11	6.25 ,,	29	6.55 ,,
15	6.32 ,,		

April

1	7. 1 p.m.	19	7.32 p.m.
5	7. 7 ,,	22	7.36 ,,
8	7.12 ,,	26	7.42 ,,
12	7.19 ,,	29	7.47 ,,
15	7.24 ,,		

May

3	7.53 p.m.	20	8.20 p.m.
6	7.58 ,,	24	8.25 ,,
10	8. 5 ,,	27	8.29 ,,
13	8. 9 ,,	31	8.34 ,,
17	8.15 ,,		

June

3	8.37 p.m.	17	8.47 p.m.
7	8.40 ,,	21	8.48 ,,
10	8.43 ,,	24	8.49 ,,
14	8.45 ,,	28	8.49 ,,

July

1	8.48 p.m.	19	8.35 p.m.
5	8.47 ,,	22	8.31 ,,
8	8.45 ,,	26	8.27 ,,
12	8.42 ,,	29	8.22 ,,
15	8.40 ,,		

August

2	8.45 p.m.	19	7.43 p.m.
5	8.10 ,,	23	7.35 ,,
9	8. 3 ,,	26	7.29 ,,
12	7.57 ,,	30	7.20 ,,
16	7.49 ,,		

September

2	7.14 p.m.	16	6.42 p.m.
6	7. 5 ,,	20	6.33 ,,
9	6.58 ,,	23	6.26 ,,
13	6.49 ,,	27	6.17 ,,

October

2	6. 5 p.m.	18	5.30 p.m.
4	6. 1 ,,	21	5.23 ,,
7	5.54 ,,	25	5.15 ,,
11	5.45 ,,	28	5.10 ,,
14	5.38 ,,		

November

1	5. 2 p.m.	18	4.35 p.m.
4	4.57 ,,	22	4.31 ,,
8	4.50 ,,	25	4.27 ,,
11	4.45 ,,	29	4.24 ,,
15	4.39 ,,		

December

2	4.22 p.m.	20	4.21 p.m.
6	4.20 ,,	23	4.22 ,,
9	4.19 ,,	27	4.25 ,,
13	4.19 ,,	30	4.28 ,,
16	4.20 ,,		

CHAPTER IX

FAULTS: THEIR LOCATION AND REMEDY

THE four tables given on succeeding pages afford a convenient method of tracing faults. It requires considerable experience to be able quickly to diagnose the cause of trouble. The beginner must not think from the rather lengthy list that a motor-cycle is always likely to be in trouble. It is only very occasionally that trouble arises.

Some riders have a tendency always to be adjusting and improving the running of the engine. When the engine is running well it is wise to leave it alone.

IGNITION TROUBLES

Testing the Plugs. If it is considered that the engine does not need taking down, yet it is difficult to start, examine the plug, and, holding it by means of the cable (don't hold the plug body with the fingers, for if the plug is defective, a mild but unpleasant shock will speedily make you aware of the fact when the engine is kicked over) so that its metal body touches the cylinder, turn the engine over by means of the kick starter and note whether the spark is regular and " fat." An intermittent spark, or a regular but weak " pin-point " spark, will render starting difficult. It may be that the plug points have become burnt, consequently widening the gap, and in this case the points should be closed. A little gauge for setting the points of the plugs and the contact points of the magneto is on the market; it only costs a few pence, and is well worth having. Failing this, a visiting card may be used as a gauge.

Sooted Plugs. If the plug is sooted or coated with a sticky black film, it should be taken to pieces (plugs with detachable centres are recommended to admit of this) and the centre cleaned with a piece of rag soaked in petrol, and the electrodes (the two points) cleaned bright with a piece of emery cloth. The body of the plug should be scraped out with a knife. The presence of a heavy carbon deposit on the plug shows that the engine is over lubricated, and the remedy here is obvious.

The Gap of the Plug Points. Sometimes, after closing the points of a plug, the rider will notice that the engine requires a

FAULTS: THEIR LOCATION AND REMEDY

different setting of the advance and retard lever to get the same condition of running as was obtained before the plug was adjusted. This is because the closing of the plug points is equivalent to slightly advancing the ignition. The converse is equally true; opening the points will slightly retard the ignition.

Defective Insulation of Plug. Don't forget to inspect the porcelain or mica insulation of the plug, the former may be cracked, and the latter may be " scaling," and a new centre (see the paragraph in the chapter on " Running Costs ") should be purchased if this is found to be the case.

Pre-Ignition. Although a plug with scaly mica insulation may appear to be sparking well outside the cylinder, the point to remember is that these " scales " become red-hot and cause pre-ignition, which means the too early firing of the charge. It may be noticed that by advancing the ignition too far a knock is caused, and pre-ignition (see Ignition Troubles) may cause a knock. A little thought will show that if the compressed charge is fired too early the gas is tending to force the piston back before it reaches the top of the stroke. When the spark is ordinarily advanced it actually does this, but beyond a certain limit a knock is heard which ceases when the ignition is retarded. The knock is probably due to the reversal of pressure on the piston head, although there are various theories to account for it. Other causes of pre-ignition are the plug points becoming red-hot, incandescence of carbon deposit or some rough part of the combustion chamber. Do not use plugs with thin electrodes (see also the note on " Pinking " later on).

Defective High-Tension Cable. It is not often that the high-tension cable may cause trouble, but sometimes, if it has been allowed to come into contact with the hot cylinder it may be found that the insulation is burnt away in one spot, allowing the bared wire to touch some part of the engine or other metallic portion and short-circuit the current. To cure this, bind the affected spot with insulating tape. Rain will sometimes cause failure of the ignition or misfiring, due to the water on the cable giving rise to a short circuit. This is comparatively rare.

Trouble with the Contact Breaker. This is not of frequent occurrence, but it must be mentioned. After running the machine for some hundreds of miles it may be found that misfiring develops at high speeds. If the plug is found to be correct, remove the cover of the magneto, rotate the engine by means of the kick-starter, and notice whether the points " make and break," or whether sparking is occurring across them. If the latter is found to be the case, it is almost certain that you will find that the points are pitted and do not make good contact, and they must be carefully trimmed with a file so that the two faces are absolutely flat. If they are not badly burnt, a strip of fine emery cloth may be doubled and pulled backwards and forwards between the points. Incidentally, if the spark across the points is large, the condenser has broken down, and this is a job which can only be put right by the makers. Whilst the cover is off, check the gap by means of the gauge already mentioned, and if incorrect, adjust them with a small spanner until the gauge just passes between them, when they are fully separated by means of the cam.

Broken Contact Spring. If you are riding and the ignition fails suddenly, it is likely that the " make and break " spring has become broken. This means that the points do not return, and quite an effective dodge to get you home is to use a rubber band to return the points.

Rocker Arm Sticking. Sometimes the rider will find that occasional misfiring, or even complete stoppage, is due to the rocker arm in the magneto being stuck. It will be noticed that this has a small bush as a bearing, and in damp weather this sometimes swells and causes the rocker to stick. The proper cure here is to remove the bush and carefully ease it with emery cloth or a file. Do *not* oil it, for even oil will cause the bush to swell.

Defective Carbon Brush. Examine the connection between the carbon brush and the cable. Beads of water or grit may be found between the contacts. It is easy to remove the carbon brush and make quite sure that the carbon is not cracked or broken.

Slipped Magneto Timing. This is caused by the slipping of the sprocket on the armature shaft, of course causing the spark to occur at the wrong time. To check the timing open the compression tap and pass a piece of wire about 8 in. long through, so that it touches the piston. Now rotate the engine, and by the rise and fall of the piece of wire and watching the valves observe when the piston is at the top of the compression stroke, and then inspect the make and break to see that the points are correctly separated.

Testing Twin-Cylinder Engines for Misfiring. When irregular running is experienced with a twin-cylinder machine, it is simple

FAULTS: THEIR LOCATION AND REMEDY

to find out which cylinder is misfiring. Obtain a long *wooden* handled screwdriver (you will get a shock if you use a metal handled one) and with the engine running, place the tip of the blade on the plug terminal and touch the cylinder with any other part of the blade ; this will short-circuit the plug so that the engine is only firing on the other cylinder. By testing both cylinders in this way one may soon observe which one is wrong, or whether both are wrong.

Another method is to disconnect the lead from one plug and start the engine, serving the other cylinder in the same way.

CARBURETTOR TROUBLES

Even on the first run the rider speedily becomes aware that the carburettor is a sensitive instrument, which soon complains when it is not correctly adjusted. The levers, he finds, must be set just so for given conditions. Even at best a carburettor is an inefficient device, and a fortune awaits the inventor of one which is truly automatic, supplying the proper mixture for all engine speeds. The writer once made a device which consisted of a sort of chamber in which the gas was mixed, the engine sucking in the properly-mixed gas direct from this chamber, It was quite successful, but too expensive to make.

The rider must learn how to detect inefficient carburation, and so to control the carburettor that an efficient mixture for a given set of conditions is obtained.

The weather has an important effect on carburation. The rider will soon notice that the engine seems to run better at night or in damp weather, and this fact has led many experimenters to try " humidifying " the mixture by injecting water spray into it—with indifferent results up to the present. He will notice that by partly closing the air, opening the throttle, and slightly retarding the ignition, the engine does not seem to knock or thump on steep hills, as it may do even on bottom gear if the adjustment is not made. The author has tried in the succeeding paragraphs to anticipate almost every carburettor trouble, and to show the remedy.

" Popping Back " in the Carburettor.
This is one of the commonest carburettor troubles, and usually occurs when the throttle and air are opened beyond a certain point, the effect being occasional popping or " spitting back " through the carburettor— a sort of sneezing of the engine. Gradually closing the air usually will cure it, but if " popping back " in the carburettor occurs when the machine is throttled down to ten or twelve m.p.h., it is a sign that a larger jet is necessary.

In changing a jet, it is necessary to see that the fibre washers are removed with the jet, as should one be left at the top of the hole and another jet be fitted, there would be two washers at the top and only one at the bottom, and petrol would leak in consequence. Petrol may leak from the float chamber if the jet is not thoroughly screwed into position, so that this matter should be carefully attended to.

Knocks and "Pinking" Due to Incorrect Mixture. Knocks or "pinking" in engines can be caused through wrong mixture as well as by mechanical defects or pre-ignition (dealt with later on). Too rich or even too weak a mixture is one of the frequent causes of "pinking," a word which in itself describes the sort of knock given forth. It is an irritating sound like a tap, tap on the inside of the cylinder, and as yet no satisfactory explanation of it has been given. The generally accepted view is that the engine gets very hot owing to the use of too rich a mixture, and at a critical temperature eventually causes the charge to detonate or explode, instead of the flame caused by ignition being slowly propagated. It is, then, *overheating* which really causes "pinking," and it necessarily follows that any cause of overheating also causes pinking.

A jet should be fitted to the carburettor of such a size that full air can just be used at full throttle. A smaller jet is necessary in summer than the one used in winter.

The Petrol Level. Too low a petrol level will cause "popping back," even though the jet be of proper size, but it is wise not to alter the petrol level without good cause. If it is about $\frac{1}{32}$ in. below the top of the jet it is correct, and further adjustment, if necessary, should be made by means of the jet.

Choked Petrol Pipe, etc. Sometimes the petrol pipe will become choked with foreign matter which has found its way through the gauze placed over the tank outlet. In such a case the rider will have mysterious engine stoppages and popping back, due of course to a starved engine. He will stop to inspect, and by that time sufficient petrol has trickled by to enable the carburettor to be flooded, so that the engine starts easily, only to stop again a few yards on. When these symptoms develop, completely disconnect the petrol pipe, and by means of the tyre pump, blow it clean, and also clean out the gauze in the tank and carburettor.

Air Lock. The cause of this trouble has already been fully dealt with, and the rider will be made aware of it by symptoms similar to those already noted in the preceding paragraph. The remedies here given should be applied.

FAULTS: THEIR LOCATION AND REMEDY

Water in Petrol. This trouble is of a more serious nature, for once water has entered the carburettor it must be taken down and thoroughly wiped dry. It will cause engine stoppage, misfiring, or " popping back." It is wise to drain the tank and use the petrol for cleaning purposes, otherwise the trouble may recur. Also blow the gauzes clear.

Carburettor Flooding. Carburettor flooding is caused by (1) leaning the machine so that the float chamber is raised above the level of the jet (refer back to Fig. 21), (2) grit between the needle valve and the seating, or (3) a float that leaks and has become partly filled with petrol, preventing the needle from seating home. Overheating usually accompanies it, when the flooding takes place whilst riding. The remedy for cause (1) is obvious ; for cause (2) the union connecting the carburettor with the petrol supply should be disconnected and the petrol drained from the carburettor. This will wash the grit away.

A punctured or " petrol logged " float can usually be discovered by noting whether its needle (the " tickler ") is sluggish in action, but if it cannot be so detected, remove the float from the needle and rattle it, when the presence of petrol inside will manifest itself. A piece of sticky paper placed over the hole after the petrol has been shaken out, or even plugging the hole with a piece of soap, will effect a temporary remedy.

Air Leak. This usually takes place between the joints of the induction pipe and carburetter joints, and binding with adhesive rubber tape will speedily cure matters.

Choked Air Vent in Petrol Tank. This is a trouble which the rider may easily mistake for air lock, or choked petrol pipe. It is obvious that as petrol flows from the tank to the carburettor, air must be able to pass into the tank, and if the vent is choked a partial vacuum is formed in the tank, causing air lock. The remedy is obvious.

Damaged Carburettor Slides and Broken Cables. Any trouble with these will present itself in the form of the machine refusing to satisfactorily answer to the operation of the control levers. Sometimes a piece of grit will become lodged between the slides and their barrel, wedging one or both of them, and causing the action to be sluggish. More often than not, however, defective controls are due to frayed or broken cables, and it is wise to get them renewed at the nearest garage ; the job only takes half an hour or so.

If the throttle wire breaks whilst riding, the standard dodge is to change over the air-slide cable to the throttle, and fixing the air-slide in some suitable position, where it is considered it will enable the engine to start easily and run satisfactorily. Don't omit occasionally to oil the cables, by detaching the handle-bar end and letting oil slowly drip between the outer casing and the cable. Stretched cables, a common trouble, should of course be shortened.

TABLE I
Engine Refuses to Start

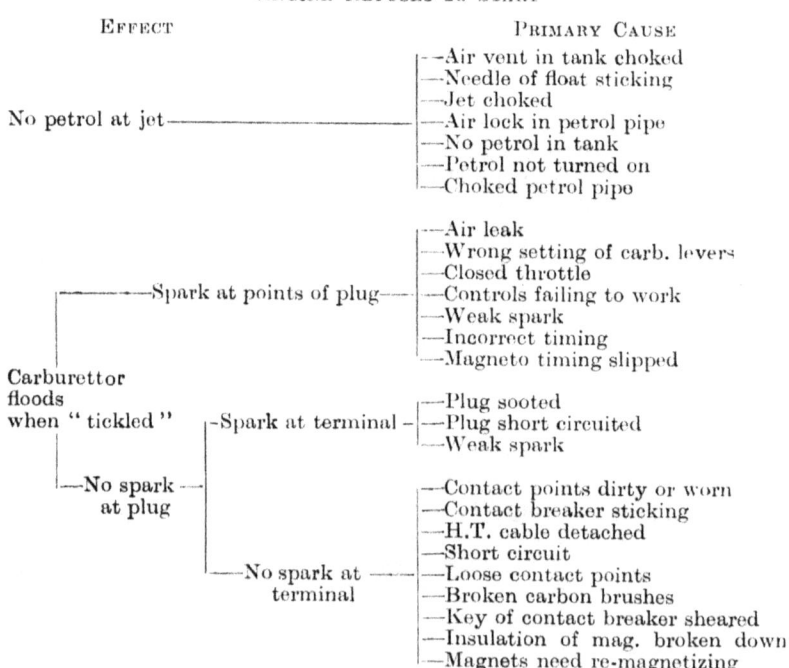

ENGINE TROUBLES

Really the troubles concerned with the engine are caused by one or a combination of the faults dealt with in connection with the carburettor and ignition, but one or two need attention and summary here.

Starting Troubles. One of the chief problems met with in motor-cycling concerns easy starting. When the engine is fairly new and in " time " it should start from cold without priming, at the first or second kick.

In very cold weather the oil between the piston and cylinder

FAULTS: THEIR LOCATION AND REMEDY

becomes congealed, making it difficult to turn the engine over at an efficient starting speed ; also the gas, passing along the cold induction pipe, condenses, so that a proper mixture does not enter the cylinder.

Piston Leakage. This is caused by worn rings, rings gummed up, or uneven cylinder wear. The rings should not be allowed

TABLE II
ENGINE STOPS

Effect		Primary Cause
Petrol supply		—No petrol —Jet choked —Closed petrol tap —Petrol pipe choked —Float needle stuck —Air vent in tank choked
Good compression	—Carburettor O.K.	—Overheating —Too much tappet clearance —Lubrication failure —Valve spring broken —Controls require attention —Air leak —Valve cotter broken —Valve broken —Wrong timing
	—Carburettor defective	—Jet choked —Flooding carburettor —Needle of float sticking —Float punctured
Bad compression		—Valve badly pitted —Valve cotter broken —Valve spring broken —Rings gummed up —Rings broken —Valve guide tight —Ring slots in line —Cracked piston —Cracked gudgeon pin —No tappet clearance

to wear so that the gap is wider than $\frac{3}{64}$ in. New rings always leak until they have worn in to the cylinder. Notable loss of power accompanies piston leakage. Where three rings are fitted the gaps should be 120° apart, and when only two are provided 180° apart. When the gaps work into line, slight loss of compression may be noticed.

Leakage Round Plug and Compression Tap. If this is suspected, place some thick oil on the seating, and observe if bubbles form on the compression stroke. A new copper asbestos washer should be fitted if a leak is present.

Broken Valve. A broken valve—which, however, is a very rare occurrence—can be detected by testing the compression, or, presuming the tappets are correctly adjusted, the stem of the broken valve will be in contact with the tappet head.

Valve Bounce. Valve bounce is caused by weak springs, which should at once be replaced.

TABLE III
ENGINE RUNS BADLY

Effect		Primary Cause
Loss of power	—Constantly	—Bad compression —Wrong valve clearance —Partial petrol stoppage —Carbon deposit —Bad mixture —Choked silencer —Wrong timing —Cams worn —Gear too high —Weak valve springs
	—Intermittently	—Partial petrol stoppage —Controls loose —Valve guide tight
Engine knocks		—Overheating —Excess of air —Ignition too far advanced —Pre-ignition (carbon deposit)
Misfiring	—Irregular spark	—Sooted plug —Water in petrol —Contact breaker stuck —Dirty contact points
	—Regular spark	—Partial petrol stoppage —Mixture weak —Temporary short circuit

Valve Clearance. Check the valve clearance when the engine is hot, to allow for the expansion. The clearance should be not less than $\frac{1}{64}$ in. An ordinary visiting card is a useful gauge for the purpose.

Valve Sticking. Valve stem may be bent, hole in guide too small, carbon deposit in the guide, or weak spring.

The Cause of "Knocks." Every motor-cycle at some time or other develops what is commonly called "knock." It is a most elusive thing to trace, and, moreover, annoying to the rider.

FAULTS: THEIR LOCATION AND REMEDY

The knock may not, as we have already seen, always be a mechanical one, but is usually caused by one of the following items: advancing the ignition; too rich a mixture; carbon on the piston getting incandescent and pre-igniting the charge (same effect as too far advance of ignition); loose flywheel (an alarming mechanical knock as if the big ends were loose); play in the big ends or gudgeon pins; magneto sprocket loose on shaft, also cause misfiring.

TABLE IV
ENGINE STOPS DUE TO IGNITION

EFFECT — PRIMARY CAUSE

No spark at plug
- No spark at magneto
  - Contact points dirty
  - Short circuit
  - Stuck contact breaker
  - Loose contact points
  - Carbon brushes broken
  - Key sheaved of contact breaker
  - Spring of contact breaker broken
  - Breakdown of insulation
  - Condenser defective
- Spark at magneto
  - Plug sooted
  - Timing of magneto slipped
  - H.T. cable detached
  - Plug broken

Overheating. Usually due to too rich a mixture, load too heavy, exhaust valve not lifting to full extent, spark retarded, lack of lubrication, excessive use of low gear, gear too high.

Hot Crank Case. Due to worn piston rings or bad compression.

Colour of Exhaust. Black smoke denotes too rich a mixture; blue smoke excess of lubricating oil.

Explosions in Silencer. Due to misfiring or too rich a mixture.

Rapid Deposition of Carbon. Caused by over-lubrication, too rich a mixture, or poor quality of petrol.

CHAPTER X

LEGAL MATTERS

THE legal matters regarding licensing and registration having been disposed of in Chapter II, it remains to deal with questions anent breakage of the law—what to do and say, and what not to do and say. It is wise to remember that the legal departments of the Automobile Association and the other clubs mentioned, are always glad to advise members who may be involved in difficulties arising out of collisions or other accidents upon the road.

Requests for advice should be made immediately the accident has occurred, and not after the case has been prejudiced by letters having been written or money having been given to other parties involved in the accident.

If representation is desired at the Court, the summons should be sent as soon as served.

What to do in Case of Accident. The first thing to do in case of accident is to obtain the names and addresses of at least two witnesses who are likely to assist your case. Take down on paper careful details of the side of the road on which you were travelling, the speed, the width of the road and the condition of its surface, the signs given (whether by hand or horn, or both), whether the other vehicle (if any) carried lights, and take measurements which may be of assistance to the case, as well as the number of the vehicle and the description. If the owner is wise he will vouchsafe his name and address without cavil, for refusal to do so may be regarded unfavourably. If an injured person is likely to make a claim, an independent medical man should be called to examine him and issue a report. Do not engage in correspondence without legal advice, or if this is not taken, make clear that all your statements in the letter are made without prejudice to your case; and refrain from making statements, either at the time of the accident or afterwards, which might be construed as an admission of liability. Do not offer money to the injured party, for motives of sympathy may be misconstrued into an admission of legal liability.

The Order to Stop. A person in charge of a horse may order a motor-cyclist to stop, and so may a constable in uniform, or

LEGAL MATTERS

a person injured by your machine. Apart from this, it is inadvisable to stop when asked to do so by others. The sign to stop should be made as already noted on page 31.

Endorsement of Licence. A licence cannot be endorsed for the first or second offence of exceeding the speed limit in the parks, nor may it be endorsed when the driver is convicted for obstruction. It may, however, be endorsed for all convictions for offence under the Act, except for first or second offence of exceeding the speed limit. It is not generally known that the holder of a licence which has been endorsed is entitled on renewal or at any time upon payment of 5s. to have a new licence free from endorsements if he has not during a continuous period of not less than three years had any conviction endorsed.

Furious Driving. A person driving furiously renders himself liable to conviction for the following offences—

(1) Driving to common danger. (See paragraph on page 30.)
(2) Exceeding speed limit.
(3) If anyone injured, indictment for causing bodily harm.
(4) If anyone killed, indictment for manslaughter.
(5) To arrest by any person, whether constable or not, who sees offence committed, under the Highway Acts.

Refusing Address. To anyone who complains that the motorist has committed an offence of driving to the common danger, the driver must give his name and address. If the driver refuses, or gives a false name and address, he is liable to fine not exceeding £20 for a first offence, and to heavier penalties for a second or subsequent offence. He may be arrested without warrant by a constable who saw the alleged offence committed, whether the constable is in uniform or not. The owner, if required, must give all the information in his power which may lead to the identification of the driver, and if he does not do so is himself liable to the same penalty as the driver.

Warning of Approach. It is compulsory to give audible warning of approach whenever it is necessary. Failure to do so renders the driver liable to conviction for driving to the common danger, and to an action for negligence if injury is caused as a result of such neglect.

Exhaust Cut-out. It is illegal to use an exhaust cut-out, or any device which enables the exhaust to escape without first passing through the silencer,

Arrest. The driver is liable to arrest by a police constable (whether in uniform or not) if he refuses his name and address, refuses to produce his licence on demand, or if his machine does not bear the identification (registration) mark.

Illumination. (See also Chapter III.) Motor-cycles with sidecars attached must carry on the latter a white light forward and red light to rear. The driver must have the identification plate illuminated half an hour after sunset and half an hour before sunrise.

Rules Regarding Number Plate. The driver of a motor-car is guilty of an offence if the number plate is not properly fixed, or if it is in any way obscured or rendered not easily distinguishable or not properly illuminated, unless he can prove that he has taken reasonable steps to prevent this, and if the driver is not the owner the latter may be guilty of aiding and abetting.

Regarding the Registration Book. When a licence is issued a Registration Book is issued to the owner, and this must be sent to the Council with whom the vehicle is registered, or
(1) When any alteration is made to the vehicle.
(2) On sale or other change of ownership.
(3) On change of address.
(4) When vehicle broken up, destroyed, or sent permanently out of the United Kingdom (see paragraph in the chapter on "Buying and Selling a Second-hand Machine").

Obstruction. Car must not be left for an unreasonable or unnecessary time on the highway.

Time Limit for Service of Summons. Unless warned at the time the offence is committed, notice of an intended prosecution for exceeding the speed limit must be given to the driver or the registered owner of the car within such time after the offence is committed, not exceeding 21 days, as the Court thinks reasonable.

Right of Appeal. A person convicted of any offence under the Motor Car Act, 1903, has the right of appeal to next Court of General Quarter Sessions, provided he did not plead "Guilty," in Courts other than Metropolitan. A right of appeal lies against an order disqualifying any person from obtaining a driver's licence.

Speed Limit. According to the strict letter of the law, the speed must not exceed 20 miles per hour on the highway. Special

LEGAL MATTERS

limits of 8 or 10 miles per hour are fixed in certain towns and villages. These must be strictly observed.

Police Traps. To ensure the observance of the speed limit, it has been the custom for the police to time the passage of motor traffic over a measured stretch of road—usually 100 yards. It was formerly quite usual for these " traps " to be located on a level stretch of road where the motor-cyclist was most likely to be tempted to " open out." The tendency now is rather to locate the " measured 100 yards " near a town or village, so that there is little or no excuse for drivers found exceeding the limit.

While the above points are given as representing the " rights " of a motor-cyclist, it must be remembered that there is nothing more despicable than the man who, taking his stand on his legal rights, cares nothing for anybody else, and *their* possible rights—legal and moral. Every right has a corresponding duty—consideration for the rights of others. It is only when the motor-cyclist is confident that he has always exercised the due consideration for others which may be considered just and reasonable that he should feel justified in harping on his full legal rights.

In the matter of offering compensation at the time for any damage caused directly or indirectly by him, the motor-cyclist may feel himself to be in an awkward situation. However, he need have no qualms on the subject. His one motive in offering the money would be a desire to behave in the right manner and to ensure perfect justice. This object is more likely to be achieved after quiet consideration on both sides than in the heat of the moment, and if the matter is going to be referred to the professional administrators of justice they particularly request that there be no well meaning interference in the matter ; for they have found from experience that such well meaning attempts to do justice are by far the most common causes for a miscarriage of justice.

It may be difficult to steer a middle course, but you will be far safer in most instances in tending too much towards an insistence on your own rights.

The owner of a motor vehicle is apparently usually presumed to be to blame. If justice is to be done in the end, the motor-cyclist need have no fear that it will be weighted in his favour—the danger lies more the other way.

This chapter contains information which every motor-cyclist should know, but once known it should be applied with discretion and intelligence. Above all, exercise consideration for the other users of the road, do nothing unreasonable and take no avoidable risks—the real meaning of Safety First.

CHAPTER XI

BUYING AND SELLING AN OLD MOUNT

Buying a Second-hand Machine. The purchase of a second-hand machine is one which should be carefully approached by the inexperienced, for so many machines with serious engine troubles which outwardly appear to be in excellent condition are available that it is difficult to detect fakes, especially when skilfully executed. Only the most reputable makes should be purchased, for one may then be reasonably assured of being able to obtain spares. A skilled motor-cyclist where possible should accompany the inexperienced.

Year of Make. First ascertain the year of make (this may be verified by reference to the registration book) by noting the engine and frame numbers.

Examining the Machine. First examine the frame for cracks, and to see that it is true. Next look to the condition of the tools and accessories, and test the head and front forks for play. The tyres and wheel bearings should not be missed, and the points of attachment need viewing if a sidecar is fitted. Having satisfied oneself that in general the machine is in reasonable condition, proceed to test the engine.

Testing the Engine. Firstly, turn the engine over slowly by means of the kick-starter and see that the compression is good. Next rotate it and listen for knocks indicative of wear. Perhaps greatest wear will be detected in the valves and valve gear, but these parts are easily and cheaply replaced. If the valves have been repeatedly ground in this fact will readily be apparent (refer back to Fig. 45), for the valve seats will be relatively wide and deep sunk, and is an index of careless use or old age—a fact which should temper one's views of the other parts. The valve-gear mechanism should be exposed and the wheels and cams carefully examined. If worn they will require renewal.

The condition of the piston and cylinder can only be gauged by experience, but if wear is detected (piston will " slap " in the cylinder when the engine is running) an allowance might be asked. It must be pointed out that a piston which slaps in its cylinder should not be regarded as a minor defect—it usually is indicative of an oval cylinder, necessitating regrinding of the cylinder and a new (oversize) piston, and it is wise not to make a purchase. There is an exception in the case of an alloy piston. This is a fairly loose fit in the cylinder when cold.

The Trial Run. After the preliminary inspection, the engine should be started and attention devoted to noise caused by worn cams and timing gears, worn piston or cylinder, or other engine noises. A trial run should in all cases be insisted on, so that one may be satisfied as to the control and general running. The trial run can easily be arranged with a combination, for the owner, if dubious, can accompany the prospective purchaser in the sidecar. If a solo machine, the owner can reasonably expect a deposit as a token of good faith before allowing the intending purchaser to take a trial run.

A Warning. The reader is advised to make quite sure that the vendor is the real owner of the machine, for if he purchases and the machine is subsequently claimed by the real owner, he must return the machine to the rightful owner and has no redress except the doubtful one of suing the vendor if he can be found.

Selling a Second-hand Mount. The foregoing information indicates in some measure the questions likely to be asked, and before taking steps to dispose of the machine it should be placed in reasonable selling condition. As such it will avoid irritating correspondence after sale, and will command a higher price than if the defects are left unremedied ; as well, excuses have not to be raised when the defects are discovered by the purchaser.

Selling Through an Agency. Several firms undertake to sell second-hand machines, the procedure in most cases being to value the machine and to allow the agent a commission on that price. As, however, such agents usually sell the machine at a higher price than the owner's figure, it follows that too high a value renders the machine of little service to the agent. Some agents even charge garage fees whilst the machine is on their premises for sale.

Selling by Advertising in Trade Papers. This is usually an excellent method of selling, because the trade papers classify the machines, so that an intending purchaser of a B.S.A. has only to look down the small advertisement columns of one of the motor cycling papers to see comparative prices. The fact cannot be ignored that a prospective purchaser of a second-hand machine buys either *Motor Cycling*, *The Motor Cycle*, or *The Motor Cyclist Review*, and this method of selling is recommended.

Advertising in the daily and local press is also an excellent method of selling.

The reader is reminded of the rules given in Chapter III (regarding the registration book) which apply when the machine changes hands. Do not let the machine pass hands until the purchase price is handed over. Beware of those who require a trial run upon part payment.

CHAPTER XII

USEFUL INFORMATION

TABLE OF GRADIENTS

Gradient.	Per Cent.	No. of Feet Rise or Fall in 1 Mile.
1 in 5	20	1,056
1 ,, 6	17	880
1 ,, 7	14	754
1 ,, 8	$12\frac{1}{2}$	660
1 ,, 9	11	587
1 ,, 10	10	528
1 ,, 11	9	480
1 ,, 12	8	440
1 ,, 13	$7\frac{3}{4}$	406
1 ,, 14	7	377
1 ,, 15	$6\frac{1}{2}$	352
1 ,, 16	$6\frac{1}{4}$	330
1 ,, 17	6	311
1 ,, 18	$5\frac{1}{2}$	293
1 ,, 19	5	278
1 ,, 20	5	264
1 ,, 25	4	211
1 ,, 30	3·3	176
1 ,, 35	2·8	154
1 ,, 40	$2\frac{1}{2}$	132

EQUIVALENT SPEEDS

Speed in M.P.H.	Time Taken to Cover 1 Mile.
10	6 minutes
15	4 ,,
20	3 ,,
25	2 ,, 24 seconds
30	2 ,,
35	1 minute $42\frac{6}{7}$,,
40	1 ,, 30 ,,
50	1 ,, 12 ,,
60	1 ,,

APPROXIMATE ENGINE REVOLUTIONS
At Different Speeds—Miles per Hour

Gear Ratio.	4	4¼	4½	4¾	5	5¼	5½	5¾	6	6¼	6½	6¾	7
Speed in Miles Hour.													
5	260	276	292	309	325	346	358	374	388	404	420	437	453
10	520	552	584	618	650	692	716	748	775	808	840	875	905
15	780	828	876	927	975	1038	1074	1122	1160	1210	1260	1310	1360
20	1040	1104	1168	1236	1300	1384	1432	1496	1550	1615	1680	1750	1810
25	1300	1380	1460	1545	1625	1730	1790	1870	1940	2020	2100	2180	2265
30	1560	1656	1752	1854	1950	2076	2148	2244	2320	2420	2520	2620	2720
35	1820	1932	2044	2163	2275	2422	2506	2618	2710	2830	2950	3060	3170
40	2080	2208	2336	2472	2600	2768	2864	2992	3100	3230	3370	3490	3620
45	2340	2484	2628	2781	2925	3114	3222	3366	3490	3640	3790	3940	4070
50	2600	2760	2920	3090	3250	3460	3580	3740	3880	4040	4310	4370	4530
55	2860	3036	3212	3399	3575	3806	3938	4114	4270	4440	4630	4800	4980
60	3120	3312	3504	3709	3900	4152	4296	4488	4650	4850	5040	5240	5440

Diameter of Driving Wheels, 26 in. For 28 in. Wheels, multiply by 0·93.
For 24 in. Wheels, multiply revolutions by 1·08.

USEFUL INFORMATION

CYLINDER BORES AND STROKES IN MILLIMETRES AND INCHES

An Approximate Guide for Comparison

A Cylinder Measuring—		Is Equal to—
Millimetres.		Inches.
80 × 80	=	$3\frac{1}{8} \times 3\frac{1}{8}$
80 × 86	=	$3\frac{1}{8} \times 3\frac{3}{8}$
83 × 83	=	$3\frac{1}{4} \times 3\frac{1}{4}$
83 × 86	=	$3\frac{1}{4} \times 3\frac{3}{8}$
86 × 86	=	$3\frac{3}{8} \times 3\frac{3}{8}$
84 × 90	=	$3\frac{5}{16} \times 3\frac{9}{16}$
90 × 90	=	$3\frac{9}{16} \times 3\frac{9}{16}$
90 × 110	=	$3\frac{9}{16} \times 4\frac{5}{16}$
95 × 115	=	$3\frac{3}{4} \times 4\frac{9}{16}$
100 × 115	=	$3\frac{15}{16} \times 4\frac{9}{16}$
105 × 118	=	$4\frac{1}{8} \times 4\frac{5}{8}$
108 × 120	=	$4\frac{1}{2} \times 4\frac{3}{4}$
110 × 125	=	$4\frac{5}{16} \times 4\frac{15}{16}$
112 × 128	=	$4\frac{7}{16} \times 5\frac{1}{16}$
114 × 130	=	$4\frac{1}{2} \times 5\frac{1}{8}$
116 × 134	=	$4\frac{9}{16} \times 5\frac{5}{16}$
118 × 138	=	$4\frac{5}{8} \times 5\frac{7}{16}$
120 × 140	=	$4\frac{3}{4} \times 5\frac{1}{2}$
122 × 143	=	$4\frac{13}{16} \times 5\frac{5}{8}$
124 × 146	=	$4\frac{7}{8} \times 5\frac{3}{4}$
126 × 148	=	$4\frac{15}{16} \times 5\frac{13}{16}$
128 × 150	=	$5\frac{1}{16} \times 5\frac{15}{16}$

FORMULAE FOR H.P.

S = Stroke in centimetres
D = Diameter of cylinder in centimetres
R = Revolutions per minute
N = Number of cylinders

R.A.C. Formula H.P. $= \dfrac{D^2 \times N}{16 \cdot 13}$

A.C.U. Formula   = 100 c.c. = 1 h.p.

A more accurate formula is the Dendy Marshall, in which—

H.P. $= \dfrac{D^2 \times S \times N \times R}{200,000}$

TYRE SIZE EQUIVALENTS

65 Millimetres	=	$2\frac{1}{2}$ in.	650 Millimetres	=	26 in.
80 ,,	=	3 ,,	700 ,,	=	28 ,,
85 ,,	=	$3\frac{1}{4}$,,	750 ,,	=	30 ,,
90 ,,	=	$3\frac{1}{2}$,,	800 ,,	=	32 ,,
100 ,,	=	4 ,,	870 ,,	=	34 ,,
105 ,,	=	$4\frac{1}{4}$,,	910 ,,	=	36 ,,
120 ,,	=	5 ,,	1010 ,,	=	40 ,,

BOOK OF THE B.S.A.

LIST OF B.S.A. SPARE PART STOCKISTS

Town.	Name of Stockist.	Address.
Aberdeen	J. Dawson	39 Thistle Street
,,	D. C. Cruickshank	13 Rosemount Viaduct
Banbury	The Central Factoring Co. (Messrs. Trinder & Osborne)	2 & 3 Broad Street
Barnstaple	Castle Cycle & Motor Works (A. S. Jones)	70 High Street
Belfast	W. J. Chambers	106 Donegall Pass
Birkenhead	H. J. Marston	50 Argyle Street
Birmingham	County Cycle & Motor Co.	301 Broad Street
,,	Falcon Cycle & Motor Depot (E. Newell)	54 Lozells Road, Aston
,,	H. Bird & Sons	1045 Coventry Rd., Hay Mills
,,	J. J. Woodgate	Small Heath Park Motor and Cycle Depot, Small Heath
,,	A. Watkins	150 Stoney Lane, and 565 Stratford Road, Sparkbrook
Bournemouth	S. Priestley	35 Seamoor Road
Bradford	C. Sidney, Ltd.	142, Manningham Lane
Bridgend	J. Lewis	35 Caroline Street
Brighton	Bradshaw's	6 Western Road, Hove
Bristol	S. J. Fair	201 & 203 Cheltenham Road
Burton-on-Trent	Campion Depot	178 Station Street
Bury	Arthur Coyle	33 Walmersley Road
Cambridge	King & Harper	6 & 7 Bridge Street
Canterbury	G. R. Barrett & Son	30 St. Peter's Street
Cardiff	Parsons & Son	2 Albany Road
Carlisle	W. T. Tiffen	Irishgate Brow
Carmarthen	W. Edwards & Sons	Towy Garage
Chelmsford	Cleale & Hadler, Ltd.	London Road
Cheltenham	Leslie Paynter	23-24 Regent Street
Chester	Davies Bros.	34 Bridge Street
Chesterfield	Cavendish Motors, Ltd.	Cavendish Street
Colchester	The Motor Cycle & Light Car Depot	119 High Street
Coventry	Coventry Motor Mart Ltd.	London Road
Darlington	Duplex Motor & Cycle Co.	8-12 Grange Road
Derby	Campion Cycle Co.	London Road
Dorchester	Tilley's	31 South Street
Dublin	T. J. Woods	42 Westland Road
Edinburgh	Alexander & Co.	115 Lothian Road
,,	J. S. Shepherd	28 Morrison Street
Evesham	Frank Morrall	Ivy Garage, Bengeworth
Exeter	Wessex Garage	61 Longbrook Street
Frome	P. Difazio	25 Catherine Street
Glasgow	Bell Bros.	238-250 Gt. Western Road
,,	Alexander & Co.	272-274, Gt. Western Road
,,	Rossleigh, Ltd.	532 Great Western Road
Gravesend	Barty's Motor Works	78-80 New Road
Grimsby	J. Plastow & Son	13 Osborne Street

LIST OF B.S.A. SPARE PART STOCKISTS—(contd.)

Town.	Name of Stockist.	Address.
Guildford	J. E. Jackson	97 High Street
Harrogate	H. Acklam	Strawberry Dale
Hereford	A. Kear & Co.	45 Commercial Street
Horsham	Jackson Bros.	London Road
Huddersfield	Earnshaw	10 Cloth Hall Street
Hull	A. E. Brown	47½-48 Witham
Inverness	Alex. Munro	14 Falcon Square
Ipswich	C. E. Hammond & Co.	6 & 8 St. Nicholas Street
King's Lynn	The " Sandringham " Cycle Works (Messrs. J. Cox & Sons)	Railway Road
Launceston	J. Wooldridge & Son	Western Road
Leeds	A. I. Greenwood	39-41 Guildford Street
,,	J. Armitage & Sons	York Street
Leicester	Campion Cycle Co.	83 High Street
Lincoln	West's (Lincoln) Ltd.	115 High Street
Liverpool	Campion Cycle Co.	70 Renshaw Street
London	Godfrey's, Ltd.	208 Great Portland Street
,,	J. Grose, Ltd.	4 Old Jewry, Cheapside, E.C.
,,	J. Grose, Ltd.	255-257 Holloway Road
,,	F. Parkes & Son	10 Sangley Rd., Catford, S.E.6
,,	Referee Cycle Co., Ltd.	332 High Holborn, W.C.1
,,	Turner's Stores,	180-2 Railway Approach, Shepherd's Bush, W.12
,,	Lovett's Ltd.	Eastern Garage, 418 Romford Road, Forest Gate, E.7
,,	The Allen-Bennett Motor Co., Ltd.	9-11 Royal Parade, London Road, West Croydon
Lowestoft	Taylor Bros.	75 London Road
Luton	Dickinson & Adams, Ltd.	Frederic Street and 33 New Bedford Road
Lydney (Glos.)	Watts (Factors) Ltd.	High Street
Maidstone	Anstey & Son	30-34 Stone Street
Manchester	Colmore Depot	Deansgate
Manningtree	C. E. Hammond & Co.	High Street
Mansfield	Campion Depot	16 Leeming Street
Middlesbrough	Pallister, Yare & Cobb, Ltd.	134 Marton Road
Newark-on-Trent	Campion Depot	46 Market Place
Newcastle-on-Tyne	Kirsop, Murray & Co.	12 Hood Street
Newport, Mon.	V. T. Waite	79 Commercial Street
Norton (Malton, Yorks)	Bower's Motor Exchange	Church Street
Norwich	H. Chapman	42 Duke Street
Nottingham	Campion Depot	Carlton Street
Oxford	Layton Garages	30 Holywell Street, 90 High Street
Perth	M. Shaw & Sons	22, Mill Street, 137 & 143 High Street
Peterborough	Burrows Bros.	57 Westgate
Peterhead	J. Campbell & Sons	34½-38 St. Peter Street
Plymouth	A. E. Snell, Mrs.	Frankfort Street
Portsmouth	Suitalls	258 Commercial Road
Preston	Loxham's	Charnley Street, Fishergate
Reading	Fortescue Bros.	1 & 2 West Street

LIST OF B.S.A SPARE PART STOCKISTS—(contd.)

Town.	Name of Stockist.	Address.
Redditch	A. L. Pitts	Evesham Street
Rhyl	H. G. Nelson	39 Queen Street
Salisbury	W. Rowlands & Sons	86-106 Castle Street
Sheffield	W. Wragg	Wellington Street
Sherborne	The Sherborne Garage (Messrs. Dyer & Sheppard)	South Street
Shrewsbury	Lewis & Froggatt	10 & 116, Frankwell
Southampton	B. B. Tebbutt	54 Commercial Road
Southsea	Percy Kiln, Ltd.	Elm Grove
Stoke-on-Trent	J. & N. Bassett	Howard Place, Shelton
Stratford-on-Avon	A. Bolland & Co.	Guild Street
Sunderland	Turvey & Co., Ltd.	Holmeside Garage
Sutton-in-Ashfield	W. Henstock	29-43 Forest Street
Swansea	I. L. Roberts	223 Oxford Street
Swindon	J. Easter & Sons	8-10 King Street
Taunton	W. P. Edwards	58 East Street
Thetford	W. & G. Lambert	Cycle & Motor Works
Tunbridge Wells	G. E. Tunbridge	2 Vale Road
Wellingborough	H. V. Briggs	High Street
Weymouth	Tilley's	The Esplanade
Workington	J. Wilkinson	43 Washington Street
York	C. S. Russell	Lawrence Street

SUPPLEMENT

1927 B.S.A. MODELS

SINCE the second edition of this volume went to press the following modifications, applying to all models, have been made—

BRAKES

All models now have internal expanding brakes in place of the dummy belt rim formerly fitted. On the 249 c.c. machine, these are 5½ in. in diameter. On the 349 c.c. side-valve and sports machine the front brake has a 5½ in. internal expanding brake, and a 7 in. rear brake. The 493 c.c. machine has 7 in.

THE IMPROVED 249 C.C. DE LUXE MODEL

front and rear brakes. The brake pedals are now mounted on separate fulcrums on all models, instead of being mounted on the foot-rest supports. All models now have three-speed gear-boxes. A special screw adjustment is provided to the gear box of all models for positive adjustment of the primary chain.

SADDLE-MOUNTING

A special saddle-mounting is now provided giving fore and aft adjustment, and permitting of a very much lower riding position.

LUBRICATION

Each model (excluding the 493 c.c. O.H.V. machine which is dealt with later), now has a new type of mechanical pump with a sight feed on the timing case. Additionally it has a control knob, which upon depression with the toe ejects a small quantity of oil on to the primary chain. In the case of the 770 c.c. and the 986 c.c. machines, the sight feed is mounted on the tank. All machines have an auxiliary hand pump, excluding the 349 c.c. super sports, which has the oil tank mounted on the saddle tube. In this machine, oil is supplied to the big-end bearings by means of a foot-operated plunger pump. Grease gun lubrication to cycle parts now figures in the specification of all models.

FRAMES

Frames have been considerably strengthened, more particularly at the head, which now has a single lug to carry the head-bearing, tank and down tubes. The frame of the 770 c.c. machine has been shortened, so that it can be used for solo or side-car work.

TANKS

The 349 c.c. machines are now provided with tanks which taper from front to rear when viewed in plan, and larger surfaces have been incorporated for the valve timing gear.

CYLINDERS

The light 770 c.c. machine has newly designed cylinders provided with deep fins and thicker walls, as well as a spring-seat saddle.

WHEELS

All models now have well-base rims and wired-on tyres, whilst the 770 c.c. and 986 c.c. machines have quickly detachable and interchangeable wheels.

SIDE-CARS

The appearance of side-cars has been improved. In several cases the nose of the body has been raised to provide a straighter top line, and side-car brakes will be fitted to order to the large touring and tradesmen's models.

THE 249 c.c. DE LUXE

As will be seen from the illustration, the shape of the tank has been altered from round to rectangular section, tapering towards the rear. The tyre size has been increased to 25 in. by 2·75 in. The tank will be finished in standard B.S.A. colours and not in black and gold, as formerly. It will have a plated silencer.

SILENCERS

These have been increased in capacity to give a quieter note without loss of efficiency.

SHOCK ABSORBERS

These are fitted to the front forks of all models.

BEARINGS

A double row of roller bearings is fitted to the big end of all OHV models.

The super-sports machine has a metal tool box on top of the tank and both 349 c.c. O.H.V. machines have adjustable knee grips.

An Entirely New Model—the 493 c.c. O.H.V. Machine, with Sloping Engine and Duplex Loop Frame

NEW 493 O.H.V. MACHINE

This year an entirely new sporting single has been produced having the following specification—

Engine. Bore and stroke 80 m.m. by 90 m.m., provided with oil sump. The cylinder has a detachable head with two large overhead valves mounted at 90°, operated by enclosed roller-bearing rockers. Special section alloy steel pushrods working in oil vapour tubes are employed, made telescopic to allow of adjustment of the return springs. Two springs per valve are fitted, and adjustable rocker return springs. A new type of timing gear embodying flat base tappets and cams with wide working faces, driven separately from crank shaft is incorporated. Steel flywheels with built-in shafts running on generous balls and roller bearings are provided. Double-row roller big end bearings have the oil fed to them direct from the pump through holes drilled in the main shaft and flywheels. An extra piston is supplied, of the high compression racing type.

Carburettor and Ignition. The carburettor is a T.T. Amac, and lever or twist grip control is supplied according to rider's requirements. A special racing magneto is fitted, gear-driven and mounted behind the cylinder.

Brakes, Wheels and Tyres. The brakes are both of the internal expanding type, 7 in. in diameter, the front being operated by a toe-pedal on the left of the machine, and the rear by a toe-pedal on the right of the machine. Wheels are fitted with 27 in. by $2\frac{3}{4}$ in. Dunlop cord tyres, wired on, and for side-car work 26 in. by $3\frac{1}{4}$ in. tyres will be fitted as an extra.

Tank. The tank is of the saddle type for fuel only, having a capacity of two gallons, and a flexible tubing connection to carburettor.

Lubrication. Lubrication is by oil sump, integral with the crank case, capacity $\frac{3}{4}$ gallon. A submerged gear pump is driven by skew gear from the mainshaft, with output controllable from the saddle by means of a valve on the suction side. Oil is supplied direct to the big-end bearing through special oilways. The visible tell-tale is fitted to the outlet side of pump, and surplus oil in the crank case is returned to the sump by a fixed scraper acting on the flywheels. An oil level indicator of the float type is provided at the front of the engine. For long distance racing a seat tube oil tank, $\frac{1}{2}$ gallon capacity, with heel operated force pump can be supplied at an extra charge. The special system of primary chain lubrication already detailed is provided. Hubs, fork links, etc., are fitted with grease gun nipples.

Transmission. The front chain is $\frac{1}{2}$ in. by ·305 in. and the rear chain $\frac{5}{18}$ths. by $\frac{3}{18}$ths in., the front chain being completely enclosed in a chain-case. The three-speed gear box has the following ratio : High, 5 to 1 ; Middle, 6·9 to 1, and Low, 11·9 to 1.

Miscellaneous Details. The handle-bar is of the special sporting type with rubber grips ; 6 in. plain section mudguards are fitted ; front having side wings and splash attachment or plain blade sports type as specified. The saddle is a Leckie Super-Sports or Terry spring seat. The silencer is plated, having over six times the engine capacity and conforming to Brooklands regulations. The frame is of the duplex loop type.

"Waysider" writes every month in *The Motor Cyclist Review.*

INDEX

A

Abroad, taking machine, 85
Acceleration, 22
Accident, what to do in case of, 98
Address, refusing, 99
Advance and retard, object of, 40
Advance, use of, 23
Advertising second-hand machine, 103
Air leaks, 93
—— lock, 92
—— vent, choked, 93
Aligning sidecar, 73
Aluminium piston, 47
Amac carburettor described, 57
Animals, unattended, on road, 32
Appeal, right of, 100
Approach, warning of, 16, 99
Arrest, 9, 100
Auto-Cycle Union, 16
Automobile Association and Motor Union, 16

B

Belt adjustments, 69
Box carrier, tradesman's, 12
Brake adjustments, 70
——, engine as, 27
Brakes, 62
——, adjusting, 24
——, oil on, 24
——, stopping without using, 24
——, use of, 23
Braking on hills, 27
——, jab, 24
B.S.A. mounts—
  2·49 h.p. lightweight, 1
  2·49 h.p. de luxe model, 4
  3·49 h.p. side-valve model, 4
  3·49 h.p. overhead valve model, 4·93 h.p. sports model, 8
  5·57 h.p. countershaft gear model, 10
  5·57 h.p. de luxe model, 11

B.S.A. mounts—(contd.)
  7·70 h.p. twin cylinder countershaft gear model, 11
  7·70 h.p. twin-cylinder de luxe model, 13
  9·86 h.p. twin cylinder countershaft gear model, 13
B.S.A. sidecars—
  No. 6, 9
  No. 7, 9
  No. 7a, 9
  No. 8, 11
B.S.A. stockists, 108
Buying second-hand machine, 102

C

Cable, high-tension, defective, 89
Cables, broken, 93
Camber of road, 31
Cam-cush drive, 44
Caps, 83
Carbon brush, defective, 90
——, rapid deposition of, 97
——, removing from engine, 64
Carburettor, Amac, 57
——, " popping back " in, 91
——, principle of, 37
—— slides, damaged, 93
—— troubles, 91
Carrier, tradesman's box, 12
Chain, front driving, adjusting, 68
——, magneto, adjusting, 67
——, rear, adjusting, 69
Chains, care of, 68
Change-speed lever, 46
Cleaning the machine, 70
Club, joining, 16
Clubs—
  Autocycle Union, 16
  Automobile Association and Motor Union, 16
  Royal Automobile Club, 16
Clutch, 53
—— adjustments, 70

INDEX

Clutch, dog, of three-speed gear, 49
———, operating, 21
———, parts, 53
———, slipping, 22
Coasting, 22
Combination outfit, driving 25
———, making left-hand turn with, 25
Commercial van sidecar, 12
Contact breaker, trouble with, 89
——— spring, broken, 90
Continental touring, 85
Controls, action of, 21
———, engine, 19
Corner, how to take, 30
——— sign, 28
Corners and cross roads, 30
Costs, 76
Countershaft gear, two-speed, 46
Courtesy, 33
Crankcase, cleaning out, 65
———, hot, 97
Cross roads and corners, 30
Cush drive, 43
——— ———, cam-faced, 44
——— ———, purpose of, 43
Cylinder bores, equivalent, 107

D

Dangerous corner sign, 28
Decarbonizing engine, 64
Decompressor, use of, 53
Depreciation, 80
Detachable wheel, 60, 62
Disc adjusting hub, 61
Dog clutch, of three-speed gear, 49
Dress, choice of, 81
Drip feed, adjusting, 23
Drive, cam cush, 44
———, cush, 43
Driving, furious, 99
——— in traffic, 30
——— licence, 14

E

Electric lamps, wiring, 78
Enamelling, 75
Engine as brake 27
——— controls, 19

Engine, cut-away view of 5·57 h.p., 59
———, decarbonizing, 64
———, elements of, 35
———, how it works, 35
———, lubricating, 18
———, misfiring, twin cylinder, 90
———, overhead valve explained, 42
———, petrol supply to, 19
———, priming, 20
———, procedure after starting, 20
———, re-assembling, 66
——— revolution, table of, 106
———, running after assembly, 66
———, sectional drawings of, 45
———, side valve explained, 42
———, starting, 19, 20
——— stops, 94–97
———, strokes of, 36
———, testing, 102
——— troubles, 94–97
———, types of, 35
Exhaust, colour of, 97
———, cut-out, use of, 99
Exhaust-valve lifter, 22
——— ———, timing, 66

F

Faults, locating, 88
Flywheel, function of, 37
Fork spring, 71
Forks, adjusting and lubricating, 71
———, spring, 58, 61
Four-stroke engine, elements of, 35
——— ———, principle of, 35
Front forks, 58, 61

G

Garage fees, 77
Gauntlets, 83
Gear changing, 22, 51
——— for starting, 21
——— ratios for 2¼ h.p. model, 47
——— ratios for 2¾, 3½, 4¼, 6 and 8 h.p. models, 52
———, timing, 59, 61
———, two-speed countershaft, 46

INDEX

Gears, alignment of, 49
———, operating, 21
Gloves, 83
Goggles, choice of, 81
Gradients, table of, 105
Grease-gun lubrication, 62
Guides, 85

H

Hand signalling, 29
Hats, 82
Headwear, 83
Helmets, 82
High-tension cable, defective, 89
Hill, braking on, 27
———, starting down, 27
———, starting on, 26
———, stopping on, 26
Horns, law regarding, 16
Horse-power, calculating, 107
Horses, led, 31
Hub, disc adjusting, 61

I

Ignition, timing, 67
——— troubles, 88
Illumination, law regarding, 100
Inlet valve, timing, 66
Insurance, 17
International travelling passes, 85

J

Jab braking, 24
Jet, level of petrol at, 38
Joints, making, 72
———, making washers for, 74

K

Knocks, 92
———, cause of, 96

L

Lamps, 16
———, electric wiring, 78
———, maintenance of, 78
Leakage, piston, 95
——— plug and compression tap, 95
Left, turning to, 29
Legal matters, 98
Leg shields, 84

Leggings, 82
Level of petrol, adjusting, 92
Licence, driving, 14
———, endorsement of, 99
Lighting-up time table, 87
Lightweight, 2·49 h.p., 1
Lubricating the engine, 18
Lubrication details, 23, 72
———, grease-gun, 62
——— system, 53
Luggage, 84

M

Magneto, adjusting, 67
——— advance and retard, 23
——— chain, adjusting, 67
——— contact breaker, trouble with, 89, 90
——— ——— spring broken, 90
———, how driven, 57
———, principle of, 39
——— rocker arm sticking, 90
———, timing, 67
——— timing, slipped, 90
Make-and-break, action of, 39
Maps, 85
Mixture, incorrect, 92

N

Night riding, 32
Number plate, rules regarding, 100
——— plates, 15

O

Obstruction, 100
Oil consumption, 77
——— on the brakes, 24
Oilskins, 82
Overhauling, 63
Overhead valve cylinder, B.S.A., 43
——— ——— engine explained, 42
——— ——— model, 3·49 h.p., 6
Overheating, 97
Overtaking other vehicles, 33

P

Paper washers, making, 74
Periodicals, 104

INDEX

Petrol consumption, 76
—— level, 38, 92
—— pipe, air-lock in, 97
—— ——, choked, 92
—— pipes, coiling, 74
—— supply to, 19
—— tank ; choked air vent, 93
——, water in, 93
Pillion riding, 26
Pinking, 92
Pipe joints, 72
——, petrol, choked, 92
——, ——, how to coil, 74
Piston, aluminium, 47
—— leakage, 95
—— ring gaps, position of, 65
—— rings, examining, 65
—— rings, removing, 65
Plate clutch, 53
Plug ; defective insulation, 89
—— points, adjusting, 89
——, reach of, 77
——, sooted, 88
——, sparking, cleaning, 68
Pocketed valves, 67
Police traps, 101
Pottering, 31
Pre-ignition, 89
Premiums, insurance, 17
Priming the engine, 20
Pump, auxiliary, 23

R

Re-enamelling, 75
Registration, 14
—— book, 100
Retard and advance, object of, 40
——, use of, 23
Reverse ; when it must be fitted, 100
Right, turning to, 29
Rings, piston, removing and examining, 65
Risks, insuring against, 17
Road, camber of, 31
—— prohibited sign, 28
——, proper side of, 28
——, rules of, 27
—— signs, 28
——, unattended animals on, 32
Roads, cross, 30

Rocker arm sticking, 90
Royal Automobile Club, 16
Rules of road, 27
—— ——, continental, 86

S

Screens, 84
Second-hand mount, buying, 102
—— ——, selling, 103
" Seizing " : what it is, 18
Selling machine, 102
Shields, leg, 84
Shock absorber, 62
Side-valve model, 3·49 h.p., 4
Sidecar, aligning, 73   [25
—— alignment, effect on tyres,
—— outfit driving, 25
—— outfit, making left-hand turn with, 25
—— van, 12
Sidecars, Nos. 6–8, 9, 11
Side-valve engine explained, 42
Sign, dangerous corner, 28
——, " Road Prohibited," 28
——, R.A.C., 28
——, speed limit, 28
Signs, road, 28
Silencer, explosions in, 97
—— : why used, 60
Skids and tramlines, 31
Sooted plugs, 88
Spare part stockists, 108
Spares : what to carry, 84
Sparking plug, cleaning, 68
—— ——, defective insulation, 89
—— —— points, adjusting, 89
—— plugs, reach of, 77
—— ——, selecting, 77
—— ——, sooted, 88
Speed limit, 28, 101
—— —— sign, 28
Speeds, equivalent, 105
Sports model, 4·93 h.p., 6
Spring forks, adjusting and lubricating, 71
—— ——, barrel type, 58, 61
—— of forks, removing, 71
Starting troubles, 94
Steering and sidecar alignment, 25
—— head, adjusting and oiling, 71

INDEX

Stockists, B.S.A., 108
Stop, order to, 98
Stopping, 23
——— in traffic, 30
———, methods of, without brakes, 24
———, warning of, 30
Studs, tight, removing, 74
Summons, time limit for service, 100
Superposed valves, 42

T

Tables—
  Cylinder bores and strokes, 107
  Engine refuses to start, 94
  ——— runs badly, 96
  ——— stops, 95
  ——— stops due to ignition, 97
  ——— revolutions, 106
  Formulae for h.p., 107
  Gradients, 105
  Lighting-up times, 87
  Speeds, equivalent, 105
  Tyre size equivalents, 107
Tanks, filling, 18
Tappet clearance, adjusting, 63
——— ———, testing, 63
Tax, 14
Three-speed countershaft gear, 49
Time-table, lighting up, 87
Timing gear, 59, 61
——— magneto, slipped, 90
——— the magneto, 67
——— the valves, 66
Tour, planning, 85
Touring, 81
Tradesman's box carrier, 12
Traffic blocks, negotiating, 31
———, driving in, 30
———, passing other, 31

Traffic pottering, 31
———, stopping in, 30
——— rules, modifying, 32
Tram, driving behind, 32
Tramcars, passing, 31
Tramlines and skids, 31
Turning to right or left, 29
Twin-cylinder models, 11–13
Two-speed countershaft gear, 46
Tyre pressures, method of testing, 76
——— sizes, equivalent, 107
Tyres and sidecar alignment, 25
———, care and selection of, 77
———, "hard," 24
———, pressure of, 24
———, pressure of, correct, 25
———, "soft," 25

V

Valve, broken, 96
——— bounce, 96
——— clearance, 96
——— sticking, 96
Valve timing, 66
Valves, overhead, 42
———, pocketed, 67
———, side-by-side, 42
———, superposed, 42
Van sidecar, 12

W

Washers, paper, making, 74
Water in petrol, 93
Wellingtons, 82
Wheel, detachable, 60, 62
——— spin, 22
——— truing, 74
Windscreens, 84
Wiring electric lamps, 78

AUTOBOOKS WORKSHOP MANUALS

ALFA ROMEO GIULIA 1300, 1600, 1750, 2000 1962-1978 WSM
BMW 1600 1966-1973 WSM
BMW 2500, 2800, 3.0 & 3.3 1968-1977 WSM
BMW 316, 320, 320i 1975-1977 WSM
BMW 518, 520, 520i 1973-1981 WSM
FIAT 1100, 1100D, 1100R & 1200 1957-1969 WSM
FIAT 124 1966-1974 WSM
FIAT 124 SPORT 1966-1975 WSM
FIAT 125 & 125 SPECIAL 1967-1973 WSM
FIAT 126, 126L, 126 DV, 126/650 & 126/650 DV 1972-1982 WSM
FIAT 127 SALOON, SPECIAL & SPORT, 900, 1050 1971-1981 WSM
FIAT 128 1969-1982 WSM
FIAT 1300, 1500 1961-1967 WSM
FIAT 131 MIRAFIORI 1975-1982 WSM
FIAT 132 1972-1982 WSM
FIAT 500 1957-1973 WSM
FIAT 600, 600D & MULTIPLA 1955-1969 WSM
FIAT 850 1964-1972 WSM
JAGUAR MK 1, 2 1955-1969 WSM
JAGUAR S TYPE, 420 1963-1968 WSM
JAGUAR XK 120, 140, 150 MK 7, 8, 9 1948-1961 WSM
LAND ROVER 1, 2 1948-1961 WSM
MERCEDES-BENZ 190 1959-1968 WSM
MERCEDES-BENZ 220/8 1968-1972 WSM
MERCEDES-BENZ 220B 1959-1965 WSM
MERCEDES-BENZ 230 1963-1968 WSM
MERCEDES-BENZ 250 1968-1972 WSM
MERCEDES-BENZ 280 1968-1972 WSM
MINI 1959-1980 WSM
MORRIS MINOR 1952-1971 WSM
PEUGEOT 404 1960-1975 WSM
PORSCHE 911 1964-1973 WSM
PORSCHE 911 1970-1977 WSM
RENAULT 16 1965-1979 WSM
RENAULT 8, 10, 1100 1962-1971 WSM
ROVER 3500, 3500S 1968-1976 WSM
SUNBEAM RAPIER, ALPINE 1955-1965 WSM
TRIUMPH SPITFIRE, GT6, VITESSE 1962-1968 WSM
TRIUMPH TR4, TR4A 1961-1967 WSM
VOLKSWAGEN BEETLE 1968-1977 WSM

VELOCEPRESS AUTOMOBILE BOOKS & MANUALS

ABARTH BUYERS GUIDE
AUSTIN-HEALEY 6-CYLINDER WSM
AUSTIN-HEALEY SPRITE & MG MIDGET 1958-1971 WSM
BMW 600 LIMOUSINE FACTORY WSM
BMW 600 LIMOUSINE OWNERS HAND BOOK & SERVICE MANUAL
BMW 2000 & 2002 1966-1976 WSM
BMW ISETTA FACTORY WSM
BOOK OF THE CARRERA PANAMERICANA - MEXICAN ROAD RACE
COMPLETE CATALOG OF JAPANESE MOTOR VEHICLES
CORVAIR 1960-1969 OWNERS WORKSHOP MANUAL
CORVETTE V8 1955-1962 OWNERS WORKSHOP MANUAL
DIALED IN - THE JAN OPPERMAN STORY
FERRARI 250/GT SERVICE AND MAINTENANCE
FERRARI 308 SERIES BUYER'S AND OWNER'S GUIDE
FERRARI BERLINETTA LUSSO
FERRARI BROCHURES AND SALES LITERATURE 1946-1967
FERRARI BROCHURES AND SALES LITERATURE 1968-1989
FERRARI GUIDE TO PERFORMANCE
FERRARI OPP, MAINTENANCE & SERVICE H/BOOKS 1948-1963
FERRARI OWNER'S HANDBOOK
FERRARI SERIAL NUMBERS PART I - ODD NUMBERS TO 21399
FERRARI SERIAL NUMBERS PART II - EVEN NUMBERS TO 1050
FERRARI SPYDER CALIFORNIA
FERRARI TUNING TIPS & MAINTENANCE TECHNIQUES
HENRY'S FABULOUS MODEL "A" FORD
HOW TO BUILD A FIBERGLASS CAR
HOW TO BUILD A RACING CAR
HOW TO RESTORE THE MODEL 'A' FORD
IF HEMINGWAY HAD WRITTEN A RACING NOVEL
JAGUAR E-TYPE 3.8 & 4.2 WSM
LE MANS 24 (THE BOOK THAT THE FILM WAS BASED ON)
MASERATI BROCHURES AND SALES LITERATURE
MASERATI OWNER'S HANDBOOK
METROPOLITAN FACTORY WSM
MGA & MGB OWNERS HANDBOOK & WSM
MG MIDGET TC, TD, TF & TF1500 WORKSHOP MANUAL
OBERT'S FIAT GUIDE
PERFORMANCE TUNING THE SUNBEAM TIGER
PORSCHE 356 1948-1965 WSM
PORSCHE 912 WSM
SOUPING THE VOLKSWAGEN
SOLEX CARBURETORS (EMPHASIS ON UK & EU AUTOMOBILES)
SU CARBURETORS (EMPHASIS ON UK AUTOMOBILES)
TRIUMPH TR2, TR3, TR4 1953-1965 WSM
TUNING FOR SPEED (P.E. IRVING)
VEDA ORR'S NEW REVISED HOT ROD PICTORIAL
VOLKSWAGEN TRANSPORTER, TRUCKS, STATION WAGONS WSM
VOLVO 1944-1968 ALL MODELS WSM
WEBER CARBURETORS (EMPHASIS ON ALFA & FIAT)

BROOKLANDS BOOKS & ROAD TEST PORTFOLIOS (RTP)

AC CARS 1904-2009
ALFA ROMEO 1920-1933 ROAD TEST PORTFOLIO
ALFA ROMEO 1934-1940 ROAD TEST PORTFOLIO
BRABHAM RALT HONDA THE RON TAURANAC STORY
BUGATTI TYPE 10 TO TYPE 40 ROAD TEST PORTFOLIO
BUGATTI TYPE 10 TO TYPE 251 ROAD TEST PORTFOLIO
BUGATTI TYPE 41 TO TYPE 55 ROAD TEST PORTFOLIO
BUGATTI TYPE 57 TO TYPE 251 ROAD TEST PORTFOLIO
DELAHAYE ROAD TEST PORTFOLIO
FERRARI ROAD CARS 1946-1956 ROAD TEST PORTFOLIO
FIAT 500 1936-1972 ROAD TEST PORTFOLIO
FIAT DINO ROAD TEST PORTFOLIO
HISPANO SUIZA ROAD TEST PORTFOLIO
HONDA ST1100/ST1300 PAN EUROPEAN 1990-2002 RTP
JAGUAR MK1 & MK2 ROAD TEST PORTFOLIO
LOTUS CORTINA ROAD TEST PORTFOLIO
MV AGUSTA F4 750 & 1000 1997-2007 ROAD TEST PORTFOLIO
TATRA CARS ROAD TEST PORTFOLIO

VELOCEPRESS MOTORCYCLE BOOKS & MANUALS

AJS SINGLES & TWINS 250cc THRU 1000cc 1932-1948 (BOOK OF)
AJS SINGLES 1955-65 350cc & 500cc (BOOK OF)
AJS SINGLES 1945-60 350cc & 500cc MODELS 16 & 18 (BOOK OF)
ARIEL 1939-1960 4 STROKE SINGLES (BOOK OF)
ARIEL LEADER & ARROW 1958-1964 (BOOK OF)
ARIEL MOTORCYCLES 1933-1951 WSM
ARIEL PREWAR MODELS 1932-1939 (BOOK OF)
BMW M/CYCLES R26 R27 (1956-1967) FACTORY WSM
BMW M/CYCLES R50 R50S R60 R69S (1955-1969) FACTORY WSM
BSA BANTAM ALL MODELS FROM 1948 ONWARDS (BOOK OF)
BSA SINGLES & V-TWINS UP TO 1927 (BOOK OF)
BSA SINGLES & V-TWINS 1936-1939 (BOOK OF)
BSA SINGLES & V-TWINS 1936-1952 (BOOK OF)
BSA OHV & SV SINGLES 250-600cc 1945-1954 (BOOK OF)
BSA OHV & SV SINGLES - 250cc 1954-1970 (BOOK OF)
BSA OHV SINGLES 350 & 500cc 1955-1967 (BOOK OF)
BSA TWINS 1948-1962 (BOOK OF)
BSA TWINS 1962-1969 (SECOND BOOK OF)
CATALOG OF BRITISH MOTORCYCLES (1951 MODELS)
DOUGLAS PRE-WAR ALL MODELS 1929-1939 (BOOK OF)
DOUGLAS POST-WAR ALL MODELS 1948-1957 FACTORY WSM
DUCATI 160cc, 250cc & 350cc OHC MODELS FACTORY WSM
HONDA 50 ALL MODELS UP TO 1970 INC MONKEY & TRAIL (BOOK OF)
HONDA 90 ALL MODELS UP TO 1966 (BOOK OF)
HONDA MOTORCYCLES 125-150 TWINS C/CS/CB/CA WSM
HONDA MOTORCYCLES 250-305 TWINS C/CS/CB WSM
HONDA MOTORCYCLES C100 SUPER CUB WSM
HONDA MOTORCYCLES C110 SPORT CUB 1962-1969 WSM
HONDA TWINS & SINGLES 50cc THRU 305cc 1960-1966 (BOOK OF)
HONDA TWINS ALL MODELS 125cc THRU 450cc UP TO 1968 (BOOK OF)
INDIAN PONYBIKE, BOY RACER & PAPOOSE ILL PARTS LIST & SALES LIT
J.A.P. ENGINES 1927-1952 MOTORCYCLES 1934-1952 (BOOK OF)
LAMBRETTA ALL 125 & 150cc MODELS 1947-1957 (BOOK OF)
LAMBRETTA LI & TV MODELS 1957-1970 (SECOND BOOK OF)
MATCHLESS 350 & 500cc SINGLES 1945-1956 (BOOK OF)
MATCHLESS 350 & 500cc SINGLES 1955-1966 (BOOK OF)
MOTORCYCLE ENGINEERING (P. E. Irving)
NORTON 1932-1947 (BOOK OF)
NORTON 1938-1956 (BOOK OF)
NORTON DOMINATOR TWINS 1955-1965 (BOOK OF)
NORTON MODELS 19, 50 & ES2 1955-1963 (BOOK OF)
NORTON MOTORCYCLES 1957-1970 FACTORY WSM
NORTON PREWAR MODELS 1932-1939 (BOOK OF)
NSU PRIMA ALL MODELS 1956-1964 (BOOK OF)
NSU QUICKLY ALL MODELS 1953-1963 (BOOK OF)
RALEIGH MOPEDS 1960-1969 (BOOK OF)
ROYAL ENFIELD SINGLES & V TWINS 1934-1946 (BOOK OF)
ROYAL ENFIELD SINGLES & V TWINS 1937-1953 (BOOK OF)
ROYAL ENFIELD SINGLES 1946-1962 (BOOK OF)
ROYAL ENFIELD 736cc INTERCEPTOR FACTORY WSM
ROYAL ENFIELD 250cc & 350cc SINGLES 1958-1966 (SECOND BOOK OF)
SPEED AND HOW TO OBTAIN IT
SUNBEAM MOTORCYCLES 1928-1939 (BOOK OF)
SUNBEAM S7 & S8 1946-1957 (BOOK OF)
SUZUKI 50cc & 80cc UP TO 1966 (BOOK OF)
SUZUKI T10 1963-1967 FACTORY WSM
SUZUKI T20 & T200 1965-1969 FACTORY WSM
TRIUMPH PRE-WAR MOTORCYCLE 1935-1939 (BOOK OF)
TRIUMPH MOTORCYCLES 1935-1949 (BOOK OF)
TRIUMPH MOTORCYCLES 1937-1951 WSM
TRIUMPH MOTORCYCLES 1945-1955 FACTORY WSM
TRIUMPH TWINS 1945-1958 (BOOK OF)
TRIUMPH TWINS 1956-1969 (BOOK OF)
VELOCETTE ALL SINGLES & TWINS 1925-1970 (BOOK OF)
VESPA 1951-1961 (BOOK OF)
VESPA 125 & 150cc & GS MODELS 1955-1963 (SECOND BOOK OF)
VESPA 90, 125 & 150cc 1963-1972 (THIRD BOOK OF)
VESPA GS & SS 1955-1968 (BOOK OF)
VILLIERS ENGINE (BOOK OF)
VINCENT MOTORCYCLES 1935-1955 WSM

PLEASE VISIT OUR WEBSITE - www.VelocePress.com
FOR A DETAILED DESCRIPTION OF ANY OF THESE TITLES

www.ingramcontent.com/pod-product-compliance
Lightning Source LLC
Chambersburg PA
CBHW070555170426
43201CB00012B/1852